THE
FORTUNES OF FALSTAFF

To

his friend and colleague

JAMES RÖGNVALD LEARMONTH

an ever-grateful patient
dedicates this autopsy of a
'trunk of humours'

THE FORTUNES OF
FALSTAFF

BY

J. DOVER WILSON, C.H.

CAMBRIDGE: AT THE UNIVERSITY PRESS
NEW YORK: THE MACMILLAN COMPANY

1944

PRINTED IN THE UNITED STATES OF AMERICA

CONTENTS

PREFACE

Apart from the Introduction and passages omitted here and there from later chapters, in order to bring them within the compass of the one hour's traffic of the class-room, the contents of this book were delivered at Cambridge in May 1943 as five Clark Lectures. Lest my hearers should weary of the names of many authorities, I reserved most acknowledgements of indebtedness for the Notes, printed at the end of the volume. I cannot hope that these are complete; for, though I have striven to present a true account, in the study of Shakespeare as in life it is impossible for the individual to recognize all that he derives from others. But my chief creditor, without a doubt, is Andrew Bradley. His paper on Falstaff is perhaps the weakest of his writings, and my thesis has compelled me to criticize it at every turn; yet he remains, nearly half a century after the appearance of his *Shakespearian Tragedy*, the greatest of modern Shakespearian critics, and we are all his pupils.

When the Master and Fellows of Trinity College did me the honour of asking me to give these lectures, my first impulse was to speak of what Trinity has done, and is still doing, for Shakespearian scholarship. It is enough to mention (i) the Capell collection in the library, (ii) the *Cambridge Shakespeare*, originally produced by William G. Clark, generous founder of this lectureship, and by W. Aldis Wright, Vice-Master of the college and, after Samuel Johnson, wisest of Shakespeare's editors, and (iii) the names of R. B. McKerrow and W. W. Greg, joint-founders, with A. W. Pollard, of modern Shakespearian textual criticism, to show what wealth and promise the theme holds. But a treatment in any sense worthy would have asked time and quiet and the use of books, all at this moment of history out of reach; and I was therefore obliged to fall back upon a subject ready to hand and, as explained in the Introduction, for some years maturing in my mind. Indeed, the views here set forth were already being advanced, in briefer and more tentative form, as three Ballard Matthews lectures, delivered in November 1940 at University College, Bangor, and their kindly reception on that occasion by Professor Herbert Wright, his colleagues and his students, did much to encourage me to develop them.

Forty-two years ago Alfred Ainger was Clark Lecturer, and his subject was *Shakespearian Comedy*. The lectures, given as I remember in a pleasant room off Nevile's court, consisted in the main of readings from the plays, and were I think never printed. But a good reader may be worth a dozen critics, and for one tranced listener that 'merry-cheeked old man' with the silver hair opened a book that has never since been closed. If the Clark Lectures for 1942–3 succeed in kindling a single reader or auditor as those of 1900–1 kindled that undergraduate, the lecturer will feel he has cancelled a small portion of what he owes to Trinity College, not only in recent honour and hospitality, but in past instruction, and owes above all to its present Master, who as a young lecturer and 'Sunday tramp' taught a group of Cambridge juniors that Shakespeare was a true historian and Clio an English muse, before going on to prove the second to the world at large by his own writings.

I hope to publish an edition of *Henry IV*, parts I and II, shortly; and I quote from that text in the present volume.

J. D. W.

May 1943

CHAPTER I

INTRODUCTION: BACK TO JOHNSON

Until recently I took my critical notions about Falstaff and Prince Hal more or less ready-made from Andrew Bradley, whose noteworthy lecture on *The Rejection of Falstaff*, delivered before the University of Oxford in 1902, still I think holds the field for most Shakespearian students. Here and there, of course, writers may be found to challenge it. An excursus on Falstaff published in 1927 is, for instance, one of the more powerful offensives in the perennial campaign which Professor Stoll wages against the romantic school of Shakespearian criticism. I have learnt something from Stoll, on the negative side, as a reference to the notes at the end of this volume will show; but for all his learning and realism the interpretation of Falstaff's character which he offers in place of Bradley's fails to convince me, as it has failed, I believe, to convince most of his readers. To write off the succulent old sinner as a stage butt, even if a witty stage butt, is to dehydrate him, even to lay oneself open to the suspicion of possessing an insensitive aesthetic palate. Thus Bradley's portrait continued to satisfy me in the main, until I began checking it with yet another portrait—that which I find, or think I find, in the pages of Shakespeare himself.

From the beginning of 1939 I have been spending such leisure moments as a belligerent world allows on the task, now nearing completion, of editing both parts of *Henry IV* for a publication known to booksellers as 'The New Cambridge Shakespeare'. And the further I go (that is, the better I feel I understand this great twin-play as a whole), the less does Bradley's delineation of its two principal figures seem to correspond with the dramatic facts. A new Falstaff stands before me, as fascinating as Bradley's, certainly quite as human, but different; and beside him stands a still more unexpected Prince Hal. The discovery is subversive; it throws all my previous ideas of the drama out of focus; and before I can get on with my editing, it has to be worked out. Such is the origin of the book that follows.

But another surprise awaited me. As what I took to be the true features of Falstaff and Hal began to emerge from the mists of preconception, I naturally turned to the history of Shakespearian criticism in the hope of securing allies; and found one, to my delight, in Dr Johnson, who seems to have observed and quietly noted all, or almost all, these features in his edition of Shakespeare which appeared in 1765. So unobtrusive are his comments that their general purport has passed practically unnoticed ever since. Yet when we bring them together, his vision of the two becomes perfectly clear, while his Falstaff is nothing allied to the Plautine braggart, which was the accepted interpretation in the theatre of his own day, and which Professor Stoll would have us suppose the basis of Shakespeare's conception. Apart from the prestige of its author, there are two points I wish to stress about Johnson's criticism. First, it was published twelve years before Maurice Morgann's *Essay on the Dramatic Character of Sir John Falstaff*, and was written, therefore, without reference to the romantic attitude towards Shakespeare's characters, of which that essay is the earliest and in some ways the most remarkable manifesto; a fact which probably accounts for Johnson's unemphatic manner—it just did not occur to him that another view of the play was possible. In the second place, most of what he has to say is to be found in a note at the end of Part II, that is, in one of those postscripts which he appended to each play as he finished it. In other words, it embodies his conclusions after editing the whole play. When I add that Johnson is the only one of the great critics whose estimate of Hal and Falstaff is based upon editorial experience, the significance of this is evident.[1] Nor will I conceal the fact that I derive considerable encouragement from it.

An editor of Shakespeare, who tries to do his duty, has, I need hardly remark, not only to establish the text and explain the language of his author, but also to imagine, as vividly as his knowledge and powers allow, every action and situation in the play he is engaged upon, as it would, or might, be represented by an Elizabethan company in an Elizabethan theatre. Moreover, through no virtue of his own but simply because there is no other way for him to go to work, he is obliged to do these things *in the dramatic order*. As Aristotle would say, he must begin at the beginning, go on to the middle, and finish with the end of the play; and he has to repeat this process, for one purpose or another, several times. It would be absurd, of course, to claim that this puts him in the position of a member of Shakespeare's audience who attended several performances of *Henry IV*, shall we say, in 1598. But it certainly protects him from the errors to which critics who have not submitted to his discipline are almost inevitably prone. One of these is the habit, which vitiates large areas of nineteenth-century Shakespearian criticism, of ignoring the fundamental fact of dramatic structure, its serial character. Thus Bradley begins his consideration of Falstaff with the Rejection, which takes place at the very end of Part II; Morgann, anxious to explain away the running and roaring on Gad's Hill, deliberately postpones his treatment of that incident, which belongs to the second of the Falstaff scenes in Part I, until he has reviewed what he calls the whole character of the man in the light of the rest of the play; and even Stoll, who professes great contempt for Morgann's sins against dramatic perspective and lays down the questionable canon that 'what stands first in the play...is most important of all and dominates the whole',[2] is himself completely silent about the first scene in which Falstaff and Prince Hal appear, and which fixes for us the relationship between them.

Closely allied with this practice of taking incidents in their wrong order is what I have elsewhere called the fallacy of omniscience,[3] that is, of treating a play like a historical document and collecting evidence in support of a particular reading of character or situation from any point of the text without regard to its relation to the rest. Being a play in two parts, *Henry IV* is a drama in which it is peculiarly dangerous to neglect the serial principle. Morgann's attempt, for instance, to establish Falstaff's claims to a considerable military reputation before the play opens, claims which have been accepted by Bradley and most modern critics, begins to look foolish when we note that practically all the evidence for them is drawn from Part II.

Scarcely less absurd are those, and they are in the majority, who, whatever their professions, in practice treat the two Parts as two separate plays. First things first, of course: Shakespeare must have finished Part I before Part II. It is probable also, since he was an actor-dramatist writing for a successful company, always eager for copy, that Part I was put on the stage directly it was ready and enjoyed a run before the 'book' for Part II could be completed and rehearsed. Part I possesses, indeed, a kind of unity, lacking in Part II, which seems to bear this out. But Johnson writes: 'These two plays will appear to every reader, who shall peruse them without ambition of critical discoveries, to be so connected that the second is merely a sequel to the first; to be two only because they are too long to be one.'[4] And I do not believe that anyone who has edited the two parts *together* can fail to perceive (1) that Shakespeare must have kept his intentions for Part II steadily in mind all the time he was writing Part I, and (2) that Part II, so far from being as one critic has called it 'an unpremeditated sequel'[5] to Part I, is a continuation of the same play, which is no less incomplete without it than Part II is itself unintelligible without Part I. In any case, the unity and continuity of the two parts is a cardinal assumption of the following study. As we shall find, it is impossible otherwise to make sense of Falstaff's character, to say nothing of Prince Hal's.

The two parts are more than one, however: they are together complete in themselves; an important point, which once grasped frees us from a serious misunderstanding. It is commonly agreed, except possibly by Professor Stoll,[6] that in studying the character of Falstaff, *The Merry Wives of Windsor* may be left out of account, that play being indubitably 'an unpremeditated sequel', the hero of which is made to bear the name of Falstaff primarily for reasons of theatrical expediency, not of dramatic art. But no one since Johnson seems to have observed that the account of Falstaff's death in *Henry V* is equally irrelevant to our conception of Falstaff in *Henry IV*, and probably, as I shall later suggest, for precisely the same reason. To point out that no spectator of *Henry IV* could possibly anticipate what was to happen to Falstaff in *Henry V* would seem superfluous, were it not that chronological matters of this kind are commonly ignored by our omniscient critics. In this instance, however, they have even less excuse than usual, inasmuch as Shakespeare has explicitly warned them in the Epilogue to Part II to expect something quite different. Here is Johnson's note in *Henry V* upon the famous obituary notice by Mistress Quickly:

Such is the end of Falstaff, from whom Shakespeare had promised us in his epilogue to *Henry IV* that we should receive more entertainment. ...But whether he could contrive no train of adventures suitable to his character, or could match him with no companions likely to quicken his humour, or could open no new vein of pleasantry, and was afraid to continue the same strain lest it should not find the same reception, he has here for ever discarded him, and made haste to dispatch him.

After which he proceeds, in one of those self-revealing passages which often delight us in his notes on Shakespeare:

Let meaner authours learn from this example, that it is dangerous to sell the bear which is yet not hunted, to promise to the publick what they have not written.[7]

At the end of this book I shall put forward another explanation of Shakespeare's change of plan. But in whatever manner we account for it, change of plan there was, and such are the terms in which the death of Falstaff should be discussed. The Tragedy of Sir John Falstaff, with which we have been so often regaled of late, is not to be found in the play before us, and need no longer engage our attention.

Johnson's views about *Henry IV* are, then, the more worthy of respect that he acquired them by studying the play, both parts of it, in the right order and for a purpose which involves close attention to its action, scene by scene. He was equally fortunate, I have said, in being, constitutionally and by accident of date, immune to romantic influence. Modern Shakespearian criticism draws much of its life from two great pioneers of that school, writing independently and at different times, each of whom labours under his special form of myopia, though it would be difficult to say which form is the more disabling to anyone examining this particular play. The critic of to-day, being heir to both writers, commonly inherits both handicaps. Behind the façade of Bradley's essay on Falstaff, for all its appearance of logic and coherence, lie the republicanism of Hazlitt and the sentimentalism of Maurice Morgann.

Every reader of Hazlitt has now come to make allowances for what Professor Elton calls 'the astonishing gusts of political fury' that 'sweep over his pages amidst the most innocent literary criticism'.[8] One such bitter gust,

> as sudden
> As flaws congealéd in the spring of day,

may be encountered at the opening of the essay on *Henry V* in his *Characters of Shakespeare's Plays.* All is calm and bright in the previous section. 'The characters of Hotspur and Prince Henry are two of the most beautiful and dramatic...that were ever drawn'; and though Hotspur is preferred to Hal on the ground 'that we never could forgive the Prince's treatment of Falstaff', the reflection is rather playful than seriously intended. Turn the page, however, and we are met with a hail-storm of abuse, directed at the devoted head of Henry V, but embracing also his conduct as Prince of Wales. He is 'fond of war and low company—we know little else of him'; he is 'careless, dissolute, and ambitious—idle or doing mischief'; in private, he has 'no idea of the common decencies of life'; in public affairs, he has 'no idea of any rule of right or wrong but brute force'—and so on for a paragraph of considerable length, until, all passion spent, Hazlitt as suddenly and almost apologetically returns to business as a critic, with 'So much for the politics of this play, now for the poetry'. It is easy to see what happened. Shakespeare's *Henry V* stands for everything that Hazlitt most hated in politics: absolute monarchy, the feudal system, the military virtues, the conquest of his beloved France, above all, perhaps, the conservative Englishman. The realization of this swept over him upon reading the play, especially as he read the speeches of the Archbishop of Canterbury at the beginning of it, and carried him off his feet. Yet this paragraph, no less an immediate product of French revolutionary ideas and hatred for the Holy Alliance than Shelley's almost contemporaneous *Prometheus Unbound*, is the origin of all later aesthetic criticism of Prince Hal. Reinforced by the reigning pacifism of the early twentieth century, it inspired an extraordinary outburst in a widely read book on Shakespeare by Mr Masefield in 1911, still quoted with approval in some serious quarters.[9] Most important of all, it was adopted a little earlier, in a more temperate and therefore more persuasive form, by Andrew Bradley, made use of to explain Falstaff's dismissal, and thus became one of the foundations of his critical edifice.

Shakespeare lived in the world of Plato and St Augustine; since the French Revolution we have been living in the world of Rousseau; and this fact lays many traps of misunderstanding for unsuspecting readers, of which the foregoing is a particular instance. And of all the plays, those dealing with historical or political themes are most liable to be thus misread. But Dr Johnson still lived in Shakespeare's world, a world which was held together, and could only be held together, by authority based on and working through a carefully preserved gradation of rank. He was never tired of proclaiming the virtues of the Principle of Subordination, a principle which lies at the root of Plato's *Republic* and finds magnificent rhetorical expression in the speech on Degree which Shakespeare gives his Ulysses. Johnson's views on

the political plays, the greatest of which is *Henry IV*, merit therefore our most careful attention, since the chances are that, sharing
as he did Shakespeare's political assumptions, he will understand
his intentions better than we do.

What then does he write about this Prince of Wales, who
seems to modern critics so ready 'to use other people as a means
to his own ends'[10], so common, selfish and without feeling,[11] so
priggish and so calculating,[12] or—to put a rather finer point upon
it—so typical of the militant Englishmen who founded the Empire
in India, 'not less daringly sagacious and not more delicately
scrupulous' than they?[13] Johnson's words show him to be completely unconscious of these sinister qualities:

> The prince, [he writes] who is the hero both of the comick and tragick
> part, is a young man of great abilities and violent passions, whose senti-
> ments are right, though his actions are wrong; whose virtues are obscured
> by negligence, and whose understanding is dissipated by levity. In his
> idle hours he is rather loose than wicked, and when the occasion forces
> out his latent qualities, he is great without effort, and brave without
> tumult. The trifler is roused into a hero, and the hero again reposes in the
> trifler. The character is great, original, and just.[14]

Perusing the play 'without ambition of critical discoveries', he
clearly accepted the story at its face value: as a dramatic account
of the unregenerate youth of one of the greatest of English kings.
The idea of looking below the surface never presented itself to
him. Above all he thought of Hal as a prince, that is, as a being
differing not only in rank but almost in kind from other men.
Such ideas may be, or may have seemed to the nineteenth century,
old-fashioned, but they are not primitive. There was nothing
primitive in the mind of the President of the Literary Club.

Rather it is the outlook of critics in the succeeding age to his
which is primitive, displaying as it does a complete lack of balance
in its dealings with Shakespearian character. The advent of roman-
ticism stimulated the interest in individual human personality to
such a degree that it came to exclude practically every other
consideration. The first manifestation of this tendency in the

criticism of Shakespeare to catch public attention was Coleridge's study of the character of Hamlet, but it was earlier exhibited in all its splendour and extravagance in Maurice Morgann's *Essay on Falstaff*, from whom Bradley directly inherited it. Its theoretic basis has, indeed, never been more clearly expressed than in Morgann's remark that the characters of Shakespeare, being 'whole, and as it were original, while those of almost all other writers are mere imitation', may be fitly considered 'rather as Historic than Dramatic beings', and their conduct accounted for 'from the *whole* of character, from general principles, from latent motives, and from policies not avowed'.[15] The trouble is that, when a critic has himself to supply latent motives and policies not avowed by his author, he is usually driven to go to himself for them. That Coleridge unpacked his own heart and intellect to account for the conduct of Hamlet is now generally acknowledged. Much the same thing has happened in the case of Falstaff, with the additional complication that through identifying themselves with the alluring old scoundrel many Victorian critics have found a vicarious outlet for their own repressions. The point is well brought out by that excellent and unassuming writer, John Bailey, who is himself a disciple of Johnson. After noting that humour tends to 'dissolve morality' and having cited the delight we derive from that 'abominable old woman' Mrs Gamp as an example of this, he continues:

Nobody exactly likes Mrs Gamp: we all love Falstaff. Why? Not only because Falstaff is greater than Mrs Gamp, but because she is a figure which we see in the street and he is a figure we find in the looking-glass. It is a magnifying glass, no doubt, but still what it shows us is ourselves. Ourselves, not as we are, but as we can fancy we might have been; expanded, exalted, extended in every direction of bodily life, all the breadth and depth and height of it. Not a man of us but is conscious in himself of some seed that might have grown into Falstaff's joyous and victorious pleasure in the life of the senses. There we feel, but for the grace of God, and but for our own inherent weakness and stupidity, go we.[16]

This is profoundly observed, and has a relevance to the attraction of Falstaff for the modern mind which I must return to later. What it tells us about his critics seems at first innocuous enough. In similar fashion, it might be said, the writers of crime stories were fulfilling, in the days of our uneasy peace, a beneficial social function by furnishing starved intellectuals with an innocent vent for their inhibited tendencies to violence. Here, however, we are concerned not with the health of the state but with the sanity of criticism; and that Shakespearian critics should make use of Shakespeare's characters as a means of personal purgation may lead, and does lead, to grave lapses of critical judgement. While some traits in a character, for example, are welcomed for the sense of expansion they afford, others may be of a kind that the critic would not desire to associate with himself, in which case they are denied or unconsciously suppressed. To quote Bailey again: Falstaff is 'a being so overflowing with an inexhaustible fountain of life and humanity that they [the critics] love him and enter into him and become themselves so much a part of him that they are ready to explain away his vices as we all explain away our own....For men of more than ordinary susceptibility to intellectual pleasure Shakespeare has in Falstaff provided a too intoxicating banquet.' And he names Morgann and Bradley as special instances of subtle persons so seduced.

Nor is this all. As the nineteenth century went on, the art of Shakespeare came more and more to be regarded as that of a painter of literary or quasi-historical portraits, or rather as furnishing the materials, seldom unhappily quite complete, for the construction of such portraits by his critics. Characters were studied, as we have seen, apart from their dramatic context, and attention to the details and necessities of dramatic structure went out of fashion. And so, not only were features unattractive to the writer eliminated; but his absorption in the problems of character often caused him to overlook incidents in the story and elements of the plot. For both these reasons, as well as others, critics of *Henry IV* have tended to concentrate upon Part I and pass lightly over the events of Part II. Even Bradley, who is far too honest a man wittingly to shut his eyes to anything he finds in a text, seems to write of what he calls 'the repellent traits in Falstaff's character' revealed in Part II as if they had been added more or less mechanically by Shakespeare in order to engineer the rejection of the real Falstaff, as revealed by Part I. And, though he carefully notes most of the traits in question, he misses others, pleasant as well as unpleasant, and those not the least important for the understanding of Shakespeare's purposes.

As a consequence of all this, the criticism of *Henry IV* flounders. Hal is at once Shakespeare's ideal prince and a repulsive sort of person; Falstaff, the merriest and one of the most fascinating characters in literature, whom Shakespeare teaches us all to revel in, is nevertheless in the end brutally cast into prison, and later dies of a broken heart; and yet the play is clearly intended to finish off on a happy note. How are these things to be explained? Baffled by their failure to make sense of the play, the critics take refuge in the theory that Shakespeare's intentions have miscarried. It is done very tactfully, of course. 'In the Falstaff scenes,' Bradley tells us, 'he overshot his mark. He created so extraordinary a being, and fixed him so firmly on his intellectual throne, that when he sought to dethrone him he could not.'[17] Or, in the blunter words of Professor Charlton: 'There appears to be no escape from the fact. This huge mass of flesh, this Sir John, has distorted the drift of the historic story and of the deliberate plan of Shakespeare's play. He has converted an intended hero into a heartless politician, and a happy ending into a revolting conclusion. How is such a critical predicament to be avoided?'[18] The answer, as Bailey saw, is that the predicament, of which Johnson was totally unaware and which is likewise invisible in the theatre, has been created by the critics themselves. It is they, and not Shakespeare, who have been swept off their feet by Falstaff. Bewitched by the old rascal, they have contracted the disease of not listening to the play, even the malady of not marking all the actions he himself performs. No modern critic, as far as I know, has ever been to the trouble of furnishing a straightforward account either of the main features of Falstaff's character or of what actually takes place in the comic under-plot; they have been too busy expressing their own sense of enjoyment and emancipation.

Look, for example, on this picture and on this; first Bradley's:

'Happy' is too weak a word; he is in bliss, and we share his glory.... The bliss of freedom gained in humour is the essence of Falstaff. His humour is not directed only or chiefly against obvious absurdities; he is the enemy of everything that would interfere with his ease, and therefore of everything serious, and especially of everything respectable and moral. For these things impose limits and obligations, and make us the subjects of old father antic the law, and the categorical imperative, and our station and its duties, and conscience, and reputation, and other people's opinions, and all sorts of nuisances. I say he is therefore their enemy; but I do him wrong; to say that he is their enemy implies that he regards them as serious and recognises their power, when in truth he refuses to recognise them at all. They are all to him absurd; and to reduce a thing *ad absurdum* is to reduce it to nothing and to walk about free and rejoicing.[19]

And now Johnson's:

But Falstaff, unimitated, unimitable Falstaff, how shall I describe thee? Thou compound of sense and vice; of sense which may be admired but not esteemed, of vice which may be despised but hardly detested. Falstaff is a character loaded with faults, and with those faults which naturally produce contempt. He is a thief, and a glutton, a coward, and a boaster, always ready to cheat the weak, and prey upon the poor; to terrify the timorous and insult the defenceless. At once obsequious and malignant, he satirises in their absence those whom he lives by flattering. He is familiar with the prince only as an agent of vice, but of this familiarity he is so proud as not only to be supercilious and haughty with common men, but to think his interest of importance to the duke of Lancaster. Yet the man thus corrupt, thus despicable, makes himself necessary to the prince that despises him, by the most pleasing of all qualities, perpetual gaiety, by an unfailing power of exciting laughter, which is the more freely indulged, as his wit is not of the splendid or ambitious kind, but consists in easy escapes and sallies of levity, which make sport but raise no envy. It must be observed that he is stained with no enormous or sanguinary crimes, so that his licentiousness is not so offensive but that it may be borne for his mirth.[20]

Both tributes are excellent in their way, for they come from great spirits; but how different the spirits are, and how little do we learn from the first as compared with the second! Johnson's words form a complete and rounded little critical essay, giving us all he has to say about Falstaff; Bradley's are merely a representative passage from a long discourse—there is a good deal more of the same kind. Yet Johnson's seven sentences tell us more about Shakespeare's Falstaff, as exhibited in the two parts of *Henry IV*, than is to be found in Bradley's twenty-seven eloquent pages. Indeed, the subject that engages Bradley, it will be observed, is not Falstaff at all, but the effect of Falstaff upon himself; upon that shy, gentle, refined, subtle, hypersensitive, entirely moral, almost other-worldly personality, at once donnish, a little old-maidish, and extraordinarily winning, that I can even now see in my mind's eye standing before me, with his frail figure and tender smile. The reference to 'the categorical imperative' is enough by itself to betray the friend of Jowett and the Fellow of Balliol.

To Johnson, on the other hand, the contemplation of Falstaff afforded no dream-compensations: the character was far too much like his own! In bulk[21]—it is one of the surprises of Boswell that he never reports Johnson as quoting 'I have more flesh than another man, and therefore more frailty'; in his love, I should say passion, for the pleasures of the table; in his fluctuation between the moods of sloth and agility; in his clubbableness and natural assumption of leadership in company with other men; in his freedom from cant;[22] in his intellectual brilliance; above all, in his talking for victory, and the unexpected twists and turns of his wit, Johnson bears a remarkable likeness to Falstaff, and certainly resembles him more closely than any other Shakespearian critic. Well might he have said: 'There but for the grace of God, go I.'

But unlike Bradley he would have no desire to run after and beg a share in his glory. He had a glory of his own, enough and to spare, at the Club; and he would have treated talk about 'the bliss of freedom' with the utmost contempt. He knew, no man better, that freedom from 'limits and obligations', from subjection to 'old father antic the law' and the restrictions imposed by 'our station and its duties, and conscience, and reputation, and other people's opinions' would mean not bliss but hell. For he had only to look into his own conscience to realize (as he did, how often!) that if that belt broke, his very guts would fall about his knees. Yet just for these reasons, not Falstaff's character, but *the play about him* would arrest him with an extraordinary fascination. 'None of Shakespeare's plays are more read than the first and second parts of *Henry the Fourth*' are the opening words of the postscript I am quoting from, and they sound like a personal confession. Here, in the mirror of Shakespeare's art, he might watch a being with features like his own, horribly like his own, subject to similar temptations, though in other times and in different circumstances, and come to a shipwreck of his fortunes that might so easily have been his too. His main interest would be Falstaff's actions, the response of his character to fresh situations; and the way the whole thing is shaped by the poet–dramatist. This is borne out by the fact that his character-sketch is largely a catalogue of Falstaff's actions; a remarkably complete catalogue, obviously carefully compiled, and embracing both parts of the play, since to Johnson the Falstaff in Part I and the Falstaff in Part II are one and the same creature.

But these things, it will be said, only go to show that Johnson, who always applies his eighteenth-century moral yardstick to Shakespeare, had personal reasons for doing so in this play, though it is of all Shakespearian dramas the least amenable to such treatment. True, he has his little sermon to deliver on *Henry IV* as on other plays. The postscript concludes as follows:

The moral to be drawn from this representation is that no man is more dangerous than he that with a will to corrupt hath the power to please; and that neither wit nor honesty ought to think themselves safe with such company when they see Harry seduced by Falstaff.

True, too, that while he breathed much the same political atmosphere as Shakespeare, the ethical ideals of 1765 were not the same as those of 1598. Yet even here Johnson points us in the right direction.[23] *Henry IV* was certainly intended to convey a moral. It is, in fact, Shakespeare's great morality play, as I shall try to show in the next chapter.

CHAPTER II

THE FALSTAFF MYTH

Let me make one thing quite clear: this book has no claim to be an introduction to, still less a commentary on, the enormous twin-drama in which Falstaff stands out as the most conspicuous figure. *Henry IV*, a play much neglected by both actors and critics, offers to our view the broadest, the most varied, and in some ways the richest champaign in Shakespeare's extensive empire. Much of this, and not the least alluring stretches, must be ignored in what follows, or barely glanced at; Glendower's domain[1] in Part I, for example. Many characters can hardly be touched; I shall have little to say about Ancient Pistol or Mistress Quickly, Hotspur or Prince John. The more subtle aspects of the play, its poetry, its dramatic light and shade, what may be called its atmospheric effects; all matters of first importance to anyone concerned in tracing the development of Shakespeare's art in the crucial and largely unexplored period that divides *Richard II* from *Hamlet*: these also lie beyond my present scope. The task I have set before me is at once narrow and simple. I am attempting to discover what Professor Charlton has called 'the deliberate plan of Shakespeare's play' and, if such a plan existed, how far he succeeded in carrying it into execution.

My title, *The Fortunes of Falstaff*, will suggest the method to be followed. I propose to look for the outlines of Shakespeare's scheme by tracing the career of the knight of Eastcheap. This does not mean that I think him of greater structural consequence than Prince Hal. On the contrary, Falstaff's career is dependent upon Hal's favour, and Hal's favour is determined by that young man's attitude towards his responsibilities as heir to the throne of England. Yet if the Prince's choice spans the play like a great arch, it is Falstaff and his affairs that cover most of the ground.

The title I have selected has, moreover, the convenience of comprising the fortunes, or misfortunes, of the fat rogue outside the pages of Shakespeare. There are, for instance, his pre-natal adventures. He tells us that he 'was born about three of the clock in the afternoon, with a white head and something of a round belly'; but all the world now knows that he was walking the boards in an earlier, pre-Shakespearian, incarnation, as a comic travesty of Sir John Oldcastle, the famous Lollard leader, who was historically a friend and fellow-soldier of Prince Hal in the reign of Henry IV, but was burnt as a heretic by the same prince when he became King Henry V. He still retained the name Oldcastle, as is also well known, in the original version of Shakespeare's play; until the company discovered, or were forcibly reminded, that the wife of the proto-protestant martyr they were guying on the public stage was the revered ancestress of the Cobhams, powerful lords at Elizabeth's court. Worse still, one of these lords was not only of strongly protestant bent, but also, as Lord Chamberlain, actually Shakespeare's official controller. Hasty changes in the prompt-book became necessary. How far they extended beyond a mere alteration of names can never be determined, though it seems possible that references to some of Oldcastle's historical or legendary characteristics would require modification. It is even more likely (as Alfred Ainger was, I believe, the first to point out)[2] that traces of Lollardry may still be detected in Falstaff's frequent resort to scriptural phraseology and in his affectation of an uneasy conscience. Of this I shall have something to say later.

First of all, however, I wish to deal with Falstaff's ancestral fortunes of a different kind. As he shares these to a large extent with Prince Hal, a consideration of them should prove helpful in bringing out the main lines of the plot which it is our object to discover.

RIOT AND THE PRODIGAL PRINCE

Falstaff may be the most conspicuous, he is certainly the most fascinating, character in *Henry IV*, but all critics are agreed, I believe, that the technical centre of the play is not the fat knight but the lean prince. Hal links the low life with the high life, the scenes at Eastcheap with those at Westminster, the tavern with the battlefield; his doings provide most of the material for both Parts, and with him too lies the future, since he is to become Henry V, the ideal king, in the play that bears his name; finally, the mainspring of the dramatic action is the choice I have already spoken of, the choice he is called upon to make between Vanity and Government, taking the latter in its accepted Tudor meaning, which includes Chivalry or prowess in the field, the theme of Part I, and Justice, which is the theme of Part II. Shakespeare, moreover, breathes life into these abstractions by embodying them, or aspects of them, in prominent characters, who stand, as it were, about the Prince, like attendant spirits: Falstaff typifying Vanity in every sense of the word, Hotspur Chivalry, of the old anarchic kind, and the Lord Chief Justice the Rule of Law or the new ideal of service to the state.[3]

Thus considered, Shakespeare's *Henry IV* is a Tudor version of a time-honoured theme, already familiar for decades, if not centuries, upon the English stage. Before its final secularization in the first half of the sixteenth century, our drama was concerned with one topic, and one only: human salvation. It was a topic that could be represented in either of two ways: (i) historically, by means of miracle plays, which in the Corpus Christi cycles unrolled before spectators' eyes the whole scheme of salvation from the Creation to the Last Judgement; or (ii) allegorically, by means of morality plays, which exhibited the process of salvation in the individual soul on its road between birth and death, beset with the snares of the World or the wiles of the Evil One. In both kinds the forces of iniquity were allowed full play upon the stage, including a good deal of horse-play, provided they were brought to nought, or safely locked up in Hell, at the end. Salvation remains the supreme interest, however many capers the Devil and his Vice may cut on Everyman's way thither, and always the powers of darkness are withstood, and finally overcome, by the agents of light. But as time went on the religious drama tended to grow longer and more elaborate, after the encyclopaedic fashion of the middle ages, and such development invited its inevitable reaction. With the advent of humanism and the early Tudor court, morality plays became tedious and gave place to lighter and much shorter moral interludes dealing, not with human life as a whole, but with youth and its besetting sins.

An early specimen, entitled *Youth*[4] and composed about 1520, may be taken as typical of the rest. The plot, if plot it can be called, is simplicity itself. The little play opens with a dialogue between Youth and Charity. The young man, heir to his father's land, gives insolent expression to his self-confidence, lustihood, and contempt for spiritual things. Whereupon Charity leaves him, and he is joined by Riot,[5] that is to say wantonness, who presently introduces him to Pride and Lechery. The dialogue then becomes boisterous, and continues in that vein for some time, much no doubt to the enjoyment of the audience. Yet, in the end, Charity reappears with Humility; Youth repents; and the interlude terminates in the most seemly fashion imaginable.

No one, I think, reading this lively playlet, no one certainly who has seen it performed, as I have seen it at the Malvern Festival, can have missed the resemblance between Riot and Falstaff. The words he utters, as he bounces on to the stage at his first entry, give us the very note of Falstaff's gaiety:

> Huffa! huffa! who calleth after me?
> I am Riot full of jollity.
> My heart is as light as the wind,
> And all on riot is my mind,
> Wheresoever I go.

And the parallel is even more striking in other respects. Riot, like Falstaff, escapes from tight corners with a quick dexterity;

like Falstaff, commits robbery on the highway; like Falstaff, jests immediately afterwards with his young friend on the subject of hanging; and like Falstaff, invites him to spend the stolen money at a tavern, where, he promises, 'We will drink diuers wine' and 'Thou shalt haue a wench to kysse Whansoeuer thou wilte'; allurements which prefigure the Boar's Head and Mistress Doll Tearsheet.

But Youth at the door of opportunity, with Age or Experience, Charity or Good Counsel, offering him the yoke of responsibility, while the World, the Flesh, and the Devil beckon him to follow them on the primrose way to the everlasting bonfire, is older than even the medieval religious play. It is a theme to which every generation gives fresh form, while retaining its eternal substance. Young men are the heroes of the Plautine and Terentian comedy which delighted the Roman world; and these young men, generally under the direction of a clever slave or parasite, disport themselves, and often hoodwink their old fathers, for most of the play, until they too settle down in the end. The same theme appears in a very different story, the parable of the Prodigal Son. And the similarity of the two struck humanist teachers of the early sixteenth century with such force that, finding Terence insufficiently edifying for their pupils to act, they developed a 'Christian Terence' by turning the parable into Latin plays, of which many examples by different authors have come down to us.[6] In these plot and structure are much the same. The opening scene shows us Acolastus, the prodigal, demanding his portion, receiving good counsel from his father, and going off into a far country. Then follow three or four acts of entertainment almost purely Terentian in atmosphere, in which he wastes his substance in riotous living and falls at length to feeding with the pigs. Finally, in the last act he returns home, penniless and repentant, to receive his pardon. This ingenious blend of classical comedy and humanistic morality preserves, it will be noted, the traditional ratio between edification and amusement, and distributes them in the traditional manner. So long as the serious note is duly emphasized at the beginning and end of the play, almost any quantity of fun, often of the most unseemly nature, was allowed and expected during the intervening scenes.

All this, and much more of a like character, gave the pattern for Shakespeare's *Henry IV*. Hal associates Falstaff in turn with the Devil of the miracle play, the Vice of the morality, and the Riot of the interlude, when he calls him 'that villainous abominable misleader of Youth, that old white-bearded Satan',[7] 'that reverend Vice, that grey Iniquity, that father Ruffian, that Vanity in years',[8] and 'the tutor and the feeder of my riots'.[9] 'Riot', again, is the word that comes most readily to King Henry's lips when speaking of his prodigal son's misconduct.[10] And, as heir to the Vice, Falstaff inherits by reversion the functions and attributes of the Lord of Misrule, the Fool, the Buffoon, and the Jester, antic figures the origins of which are lost in the dark backward and abysm of folk-custom.[11] We shall find that Falstaff possesses a strain, and more than a strain, of the classical *miles gloriosus* as well. In short, the Falstaff-Hal plot embodies a composite myth which had been centuries amaking, and was for the Elizabethans full of meaning that has largely disappeared since then: which is one reason why we have come so seriously to misunderstand the play.

Nor was Shakespeare the first to see Hal as the prodigal. The legend of Harry of Monmouth began to grow soon after his death in 1422; and practically all the chroniclers, even those writing in the fifteenth century, agree on his wildness in youth and on the sudden change that came upon him at his accession to the throne. The essence of Shakespeare's plot is, indeed, already to be found in the following passage about King Henry V taken from Fabyan's *Chronicle* of 1516:

This man, before the death of his fader, applyed him unto all vyce and insolency, and drewe unto hym all ryottours and wylde disposed persones; but after he was admytted to the rule of the lande, anone and suddenly he became a newe man, and tourned al that rage into sobernesse and wyse sadnesse, and the vyce into constant vertue. And for he wolde contynewe the vertue, and not to be reduced thereunto by the familiarytie of his olde nyse company, he therefore, after rewardes to them gyuen, charged theym upon payne of theyr lyues, that none of theym were so hardy to come within x. myle of such place as he were lodgyd, after a day by him assigned.[12]

There appears to be no historical basis for any of this, and Kingsford has plausibly suggested that its origin may be 'contemporary scandal which attached to Henry through his youthful association with the unpopular Lollard leader' Sir John Oldcastle. 'It is noteworthy', he points out, 'that Henry's political opponents were Oldcastle's religious persecutors; and also that those writers who charge Henry with wildness as Prince find his peculiar merit as King in the maintaining of Holy Church and destroying of heretics. A supposed change in his attitude on questions of religion may possibly furnish a partial solution for his alleged "change suddenly into a new man".'[13] The theory is the more attractive that it would account not only for Hal's conversion but also for Oldcastle's degradation from a protestant martyr and distinguished soldier to what Ainger calls 'a broken-down Lollard, a fat old sensualist, retaining just sufficient recollection of the studies of his more serious days to be able to point his jokes with them'.

Yet when all is said, the main truth seems to be that the fifteenth and early sixteenth centuries, the age of allegory in poetry and morality in drama, needed a Prodigal Prince, whose miraculous conversion might be held up as an example by those concerned (as what contemporary political writer was not?) with the education of young noblemen and princes. And could any more alluring fruits of repentance be offered such pupils than the prowess and statesmanship of Henry V, the hero of Agincourt, the mirror of English kingship for a hundred years? In his miracle play, *Richard II*, Shakespeare had celebrated the traditional royal martyr;[14] in his morality play, *Henry IV*, he does the like with the traditional royal prodigal.

He made the myth his own, much as musicians adopt and absorb a folk-tune as the theme for a symphony. He glorified it, elaborated it, translated it into what were for the Elizabethans modern terms, and exalted it into a heaven of delirious fun and frolic; yet never, for a moment, did he twist it from its original purpose, which was serious, moral, didactic. Shakespeare plays no tricks with his public. He did not, like Euripides, dramatize the stories of his race and religion in order to subvert the traditional ideals those stories were first framed to set forth. Prince Hal is the prodigal, and his repentance is not only to be taken seriously, it is to be admired and commended. Moreover, the story of the prodigal, secularized and modernized as it might be, ran the same course as ever and contained the same three principal characters: the tempter, the younker, and the father with property to bequeath and counsel to give. It followed also the fashion set by miracle, morality and the Christian Terence by devoting much attention to the doings of the first-named. Shakespeare's audience enjoyed the fascination of Prince Hal's 'white-bearded Satan' for two whole plays, as perhaps no character on the world's stage had ever been enjoyed before. But they knew, from the beginning, that the reign of this marvellous Lord of Misrule must have an end, that Falstaff must be rejected by the Prodigal Prince, when the time for reformation came. And they no more thought of questioning or disapproving of that finale, than their ancestors would have thought of protesting against the Vice being carried off to Hell at the end of the interlude.

The main theme, therefore, of Shakespeare's morality play is the growing-up of a madcap prince into the ideal king, who was Henry V; and the play was made primarily—already made by some dramatist before Shakespeare took it over—in order to exhibit his conversion and to reveal his character unfolding towards that end, as he finds himself faced more and more directly by his responsibilities. It is that which determines its very shape. Even the 'fearful symmetry' of Falstaff's own person was welded upon the anvil of that purpose. It is probably because the historical Harry of Monmouth 'exceeded the meane stature of men', as his earliest chronicler tells us; 'his necke...longe, his body slender and leane, his boanes smale',[15]—because in Falstaff's words he actually was a starveling, an eel-skin, a tailor's yard, and all the rest of it—that the idea of Falstaff himself as 'a huge hill of flesh' first came to Shakespeare.[16] It was certainly, at any rate in part, in order to explain and palliate the Prince's love of rioting and wantonness that he set out to make Falstaff as enchanting as he could.[17] And he succeeded so well that the young man now lies under the stigma, not of having yielded to the tempter, but of disentangling himself, in the end, from his toils. After all, Falstaff *is* 'a devil...in the likeness of an old fat man', and the Devil has generally been supposed to exercise limitless attraction in his dealings with the sons of men. A very different kind of poet, who imagined a very different kind of Satan, has been equally and similarly misunderstood by modern critics, who no longer believing in the Prince of Darkness have ceased to understand him. For, as Professor R. W. Chambers reminded us in his last public utterance,[18] when Blake declared that Milton was 'of the Devil's party without knowing it', he overlooked the fact, and his many successors have likewise overlooked the fact, that, if the fight in Heaven, the struggle in Eden, the defeat of Adam and Eve, and the victory of the Second Adam in *Paradise Regained*, are to appear in their true proportions, we must be made to realize how immeasurable, how indomitable, is the spirit of the Great Enemy. It may also be noted that Milton's Son of God has in modern times been charged with priggishness no less freely than Shakespeare's son of Bolingbroke.

Shakespeare, I say, translated his myth into a language and endued it with an atmosphere that his contemporaries would best appreciate. First, Hal is not only youth or the prodigal, he is the young prodigal *prince*, the youthful heir to the throne. The translation, then, already made by the chroniclers, if Kingsford be right, from sectarian terms into those more broadly religious or moral, now takes us out of the theological into the political sphere. This is seen most clearly in the discussion of the young king's remarkable conversion by the two bishops at the beginning of *Henry V*. King Henry, as Bradley notes, 'is much more obviously religious than most of Shakespeare's heroes',[19] so that one would expect the bishops to interpret his change of life as a religious conversion. Yet they say nothing about religion except that he is 'a true lover of the holy church' and can 'reason in divinity'; the rest of their talk, some seventy lines, is concerned with learning and statecraft. In fact, the conversation of these worldly prelates demonstrates that the conversion is not the old repentance for sin and amendment of life, which is the burden, as we have seen, of Fabyan and other chroniclers, but a repentance of the renaissance type, which transforms an idle and wayward prince into an excellent soldier and governor. Even King Henry IV, at the bitterest moments of the scenes with his son, never taxes him with sin, and his only use of the word refers to sins that would multiply in the country, when

> the fifth Harry from curbed licence plucks
> The muzzle of restraint.[20]

If Hal had sinned, it was not against God, but against Chivalry, against Justice, against his father, against the interests of the crown, which was the keystone of England's political and social stability. Instead of educating himself for the burden of kingship, he had been frittering away his time, and making himself cheap, with low companions

> that daff the world aside
> And bid it pass.

In a word, a word that Shakespeare applies no less than six times to his conduct, he is guilty of Vanity. And Vanity, though not in the theological category of the Seven Deadly Sins, was a cardinal iniquity in a young prince or nobleman of the sixteenth and seventeenth centuries; almost as heinous, in fact, as Idleness in an apprentice.

I am not suggesting that this represents Shakespeare's own view. Of Shakespeare's views upon the problems of conduct, whether in prince or commoner, we are in general ignorant, though he seems to hint in both *Henry IV* and *Henry V* that the Prince of Wales learnt some lessons at least from Falstaff and his crew,

Francis and his fellow-drawers, which stood him in good stead when he came to rule the country and command troops in the field. But it is the view that his father and his own conscience take of his misreadings; and, as the spectators would take it as well, we must regard it as the thesis to which Shakespeare addressed himself.

When, however, he took audiences by storm in 1597 and 1598 with his double *Henry IV* he gave them something much more than a couple of semi-mythical figures from the early fifteenth century, brought up to date politically. He presented persons and situations at once fresh and actual. Both Hal and Falstaff are denizens of Elizabethan London. Hal thinks, acts, comports himself as an heir to the Queen might have done, had she delighted her people by taking a consort and giving them a Prince of Wales; while Falstaff symbolizes, on the one hand, all the feasting and good cheer for which Eastcheap stood, and reflects, on the other, the shifts, subterfuges, and shady tricks that decayed gentlemen and soldiers were put to if they wished to keep afloat and gratify their appetites in the London underworld of the late sixteenth century. It is the former aspects of the old scoundrel that probably gave most pleasure to those who first saw him on the stage; and, as they are also those that we moderns are most likely to miss, I make no apology for devoting most of the rest of this chapter to an exposition of them.

Sweet Beef

Riot invites Youth, it will be remembered, to drink wine at a tavern, and tavern scenes are common in other interludes, especially those of the Prodigal Son variety. But Shakespeare's tavern is more than a drink-shop, while his Riot is not only a 'huge bombard of sack' but also a 'roasted Manningtree ox with the pudding in his belly'.

The site of the Boar's Head tavern in Eastcheap is now as deep-sunk in the ooze of human forgetfulness as that of the palace of Haroun. But it was once a real hostelry, and must have meant much to Londoners of the reigns of Elizabeth and James. Records are scanty, but the very fact that Shakespeare makes it Falstaff's headquarters suggests that it was the best tavern in the city. And the further fact that he avoids mentioning it directly, though quibbling upon the name more than once,[21] suggests, on the one hand, that he kept the name off the stage in order to escape complications with the proprietors of the day, and on the other that he could trust his audience to jump to so obvious an identification without prompting. In any event, no other tavern in Eastcheap is at all likely to have been intended, and as Eastcheap is referred to six times in various scenes, there can be little real doubt that what Falstaff once calls 'the king's tavern'[22] is the famous Boar's Head, the earliest known reference to which occurs in a will dating from the reign of Richard II.[23] Whether there is anything or not in Skeat's conjecture that the Glutton in *Piers Plowman* made it the scene of his exploits like Falstaff,[24] it was a well-known house of entertainment more than two hundred years before Shakespeare introduced it into his play, and had come therefore by his day to be regarded as a historic hostelry, for which reason it was probably already associated in popular imagination with the floating legends of the wild young prince. What, however, seems to have escaped the attention of modern writers is that the house, with a name that symbolized good living and good fellowship above that of any other London tavern, was almost certainly even better known for good food than for good drink.

Eastcheap, there is plenty of evidence to show, was then, and had long been, the London centre at once of butchers and cookshops. Lydgate, writing in the reign of Henry V, puts the following words in the mouth of his *London Lyckpenny*:

> Then I hyed me into Estchepe;
> One cryes 'rybbes of befe and many a pye';
> Pewter pots they clattered on a heap;
> There was a harp, pype, and minstrelsy.

The street was famed, in short, not only for meat and drink, but also for the 'noise' of musicians, which belonged to 'the old Tauerne in Eastcheap' in *The Famous Victories*, and which 'Mistress

Tearsheet would fain hear' in Part II of *Henry IV*.[25] As for 'rybbes of befe', though we never see or hear of Falstaff eating, or desiring to eat, anything except Goodwife Keech's dish of prawns[26] and the capon, anchovies and halfpenny worth of bread recorded with 'an intolerable deal of sack' in the bill found upon him while asleep,[27] Shakespeare none the less contrives to associate him perpetually with appetizing food by means of the imagery that plays about his person. For the epithets and comparisons which Hal and Poins apply to him, or he himself makes use of, though at times connected with his consumption of sack, are far more often intended to recall the chief stock-in-trade of the victuallers and butchers of Eastcheap, namely meat of all kinds, and meat both raw and roast.

Falstaff is once likened to a 'huge bombard',[28] once to a 'hogshead',[29] once to a 'tun',[30] and twice to a 'hulk', that is, to a cargo-boat; the nature of the cargo being specified by Doll, who protests to Mistress Quickly, 'There's a whole merchant's venture of Bourdeaux stuff in him, you have not seen a hulk better stuffed in the hold'.[31] But beyond these there is little or nothing about him in the vintner's line. When, on the other hand, Shakespeare promises the audience, through the mouth of his Epilogue in Part II, to continue the story, with Sir John in it, 'if you be not too much cloyed with fat meat', the phrase sums up the prevailing image, constant in reference though ever-varying in form, which the physical characteristics of Falstaff presented to his mind's eye, and which he in turn was at pains to keep before the mind's eye of his public. Changes in London, and even more, changes in the language, have obliterated all this for the modern reader, so that what was intended, from the first, as little more than a kind of shimmering half-apprehended jest playing upon the surface of the dialogue, must now be recovered as a piece of archaeology, that is, as something long dead. The laughter has gone out of it; yet I shall be disappointed if the reader does not catch himself smiling now and again at what follows.

'Call in Ribs, call in Tallow' is Hal's cue for Falstaff's entry in the first great Boar's Head scene; and what summons to the choicest feast in comedy could be more apt? For there is the noblest of English dishes straightaway: Sir John as roast Sir Loin-of-Beef, gravy and all. 'Tallow', a word often applied to him, generally in opprobrium, is not rightly understood, unless two facts be recalled: first, that it meant to the Elizabethans liquid fat, as well as dripping or suet or animal fat rendered down; second, that human sweat, partly owing perhaps to the similarity of the word to 'suet', was likewise thought of as fat, melted by the heat of the body. The most vivid presentation of Falstaff served up hot, so to say, is the picture we get of him sweating with fright in Mistress Page's dirty linen basket, as it was emptied by her servants into the Thames; and though *The Merry Wives* does not strictly belong to the Falstaff canon, the passage may be quoted here, as giving the clue to passages in *Henry IV* itself. For however different in character the Windsor Falstaff may be from his namesake of Eastcheap, he possesses the same body, the body that on Gad's Hill 'sweats to death, and *lards* the lean earth, as he walks along'.[32]

'And then', he relates to the disguised Ford,

to be stopped in, like a strong distillation, with stinking clothes that fretted in their own grease! Think of that, a man of my kidney! think of that—that am as subject to heat, as butter; a man of continual dissolution and thaw; it was a miracle to 'scape suffocation. And in the height of this bath, when I was more than half stewed in grease, like a Dutch dish, to be thrown into the Thames, and cooled, glowing-hot, in that surge, like a horse-shoe. Think of that—hissing hot: think of that, Master Brook![33]

The 'greasy tallow-catch',[34] again, to which the Prince compares him, much to the bewilderment of commentators, betokens, I believe, nothing more mysterious than a dripping-pan to catch the fat as the roasting joint turned upon the spit before the fire. Or take the following scrap of dialogue:

L. *Chief Justice.* What, you are as a candle, the better part burnt out.
Falstaff. A wassail candle, my lord, all tallow—if I did say of wax, my growth would approve the truth.

L. Chief Justice. There is not a white hair on your face, but should have his effect of gravity.

Falstaff. His effect of gravy, gravy, gravy.[35]

Falstaff's repeated 'gravy' is a quibble, of course. But it is not just a feeble jest upon his table manners, as seems to be usually assumed: it follows upon the mention of 'tallow' and refers to the drops of sweat that never cease to stand upon his face. In fact, to use a seventeenth-century expression, applicable to one bathed in perspiration, he may be said perpetually to 'stew in his own gravy'[36]

Indeed, he glories in the fact. Was it not, according to the physiological notions of the time, the very warrant of his enormous vitality? Never is he more angered to the heart than when the Prince likens him one day to a dry withered old apple-john. His complexion is merely sanguine; heat and moisture mingle to form the element he moves in; except in moods of mock-repentance he leaves to baser earth the cold and dry of melancholy.[37]

Once we have the trick of it, all sorts of other allusions and playful terms of abuse are seen to belong to the same category, while the analogy between that vast carcase, as a whole or in its parts, and roasts of various kinds is capable of almost infinite elaboration. 'Chops', for instance, as he is twice called,[38] carries the double significance of 'fat cheeks' and 'cutlets'; 'guts', the Elizabethan word for 'tripe', is an epithet that occurs no less than five times;[39] and 'sweet beef' as a term of endearment[40] requires no explaining. Nor is he only served up as beef; pork, still more appropriate to the Boar's Head, though brought in less often, provides some magnificent examples. The term 'brawn', which means a large pig fattened for the slaughter, is applied to him on two occasions;[41] on his return from Wales the Prince, enquiring of Bardolph, 'Is your master here in London?. . . Where sups he? doth the old boar feed in the old frank?'[42] refers to the familiar inn-sign; Falstaff himself declares that he walks the streets followed by the diminutive page 'like a sow that hath overwhelmed all her litter but one';[43] last, and best of all, when Doll salutes him between her 'flattering busses' as her 'whoreson little tidy Bartholomew boar-pig',[44] she is alluding to the tender sweet-fleshed little sucking-pigs which formed the chief delicacy at Bartholomew Fair.

The mention of Bartholomew Fair, the most popular annual festivity of Elizabethan and Jacobean London, may be linked with two other comparisons, which take us beyond the confines of Eastcheap and help to bestow on Falstaff that 'touch of infinity' which Bradley discovers in him, associating him, as they do, with feasting on a vast and communal scale. The first, already quoted above, is the Prince's description of him as a 'Manningtree ox with the pudding in his belly',[45] in other words, as an ox roasted whole and stuffed with sausages, after the fashion of the annual fairs at Manningtree, an Essex town famed for the exceeding fatness of its beasts. But the extremest inch of possibility is reached by Poins when he asks Bardolph 'How doth the Martlemas, your master?'[46] Martlemas, or the feast of St Martin, on 11 November, was in those days of scarce fodder the season at which most of the beasts had to be killed off and salted for the winter, and therefore the season for great banquets of fresh meat. Thus it had been for centuries, long before the coming of Christianity,[47] and thus it remained down to the introduction of the cropping of turnips in the eighteenth century. In calling him a 'Martlemas' Poins is at once likening Falstaff's enormous proportions to the prodigality of fresh-killed meat which the feast brought, and acclaiming his identity with Riot and Festivity in general.[48] But perhaps the best comment upon Falstaff as Martlemas comes from Spenser's procession of the seasons in the Book of Mutabilitie. His November might almost be Falstaff himself, though the dates prove that the two figures must be independent:

> Next was Nouember, he full grosse and fat,
> As fed with lard, and that right well might seeme;
> For, he had been a fatting hogs of late,
> That yet his browes with sweat did reek and steem,
> And yet the season was full sharp and breem.[49]

One might go to the other end of the scale and point out that the objects Falstaff chooses as a contrast to his person, objects excessively thin, wizened or meagre, are likewise often taken from the food-shops. There is, for instance, the shotten herring, the soused gurnet, the bunch of radish, the rabbit-sucker or poulter's hare, and wittiest of all perhaps, the carbonado—the rasher of bacon, we should say—which he will only allow Hotspur to make of him, if he is foolish enough to come in his way.[50] But enough to have shown that by plying his audience with suggestions of the choicest food that London and Eastcheap had to offer, whenever the person of Falstaff is mentioned, Shakespeare lays as it were the physical foundations of his Falstaff myth.

The prodigiously incarnate Riot, who fills the Boar's Head with his jollity, typifies much more, of course, than the pleasures of the table. He stands for a whole globe of happy continents, and his laughter is 'broad as ten thousand beeves at pasture'.[51] But he is Feasting first, and his creator never allows us to forget it. For in this way he not only perpetually associates him in our minds with appetizing images, but contrives that as we laugh at his wit our souls shall be satisfied as with marrow and fatness. No one has given finer expression to this satisfaction than Hazlitt, and I may fitly round off the topic with words of his:

Falstaff's wit is an emanation of a fine constitution; an exuberance of good-humour and good-nature; an overflowing of his love of laughter and good-fellowship; a giving vent to his heart's ease, and over-contentment with himself and others. He would not be in character, if he were not so fat as he is; for there is the greatest keeping in the boundless luxury of his imagination and the pampered self-indulgence of his physical appetites. He manures and nourishes his mind with jests, as he does his body with sack and sugar. He carves out his jokes, as he would a capon or a haunch of venison, where there is *cut and come again*; and pours out upon them the oil of gladness. His tongue drops fatness, and in the chambers of his brain 'it snows of meat and drink'. He keeps perpetually holiday and open house, and we live with him in a round of invitations to a rump and dozen....He never fails to enrich his discourse with allusions to eating and drinking, but we never see him at table. He carries his own larder about with him, and is himself 'a tun of man'.[52]

MONSIEUR REMORSE

Like all great Shakespearian characters Falstaff is a bundle of
contradictions. He is not only Riot but also Repentance. He can
turn an eye of melancholy upon us, assume the role of puritan
sanctimony, and when it pleases him, even threaten amendment
of life. It is, of course, *mock*-repentance, carried through as part
of the untiring 'play extempore' with which he keeps the Prince,
and us, and himself, entertained from beginning to end of the
drama. And yet it is not mere game; Shakespeare makes it more
interesting by persuading us that there is a strain of sincerity in it;
and it almost completely disappears in Part II, when the rogue
finds himself swimming on the tide of success. There is a good
deal of it in Part I, especially in the earliest Falstaff scenes.

But, Hal, I prithee, trouble me no more with vanity. I would to God
thou and I knew where a commodity of good names were to be bought.
Thou hast done much harm upon me, Hal—God forgive thee for it:
before I knew thee, Hal, I knew nothing, and now am I, if a man should
speak truly, little better than one of the wicked: I must give over this
life, and I will give it over: by the Lord, an I do not, I am a villain. I'll
be damned for never a king's son in Christendom.[53]

One of his favourite poses is that of the innocent, beguiled by
a wicked young heir apparent; he even makes it the burden of his
apologia to the Lord Chief Justice at their first encounter. It serves
too when things go wrong, when resolute men who have taken
£1000 on Gad's Hill are left in the lurch by cowardly friends, or
when there's lime in a cup of sack:

There is nothing but roguery to be found in villainous man, yet a
coward is worse than a cup of sack with lime in it. A villainous coward!
Go thy ways, old Jack, die when thou wilt, if manhood, good manhood,
be not forgot upon the face of the earth, then am I a shotten herring. . . .
There lives not three good men unhanged in England, and one of them
is fat, and grows old. God help the while! a bad world, I say. I would
I were a weaver—I could sing psalms or anything.[54]

But beside this talk of escaping from a wicked world and the toils of a naughty young prince, there is also the pose of personal repentance. At his first entry Poins hails him as Monsieur Remorse, an indication that this is one of his recognized roles among Corinthians and lads of mettle. And we may see him playing it at the opening of act 3, scene 3, when there is no Hal present to require entertaining.

Well, I'll repent, and that suddenly, while I am in some liking. I shall be out of heart shortly, and then I shall have no strength to repent. An I have not forgotten what the inside of a church is made of, I am a peppercorn, a brewer's horse. The inside of a church! Company, villainous company, hath been the spoil of me.

Such passages, together with the habit of citing Scripture, may have their origin, I have said, in the puritan, psalm-singing, temper of Falstaff's prototype—that comic Lollard, Sir John Oldcastle in the old *Henry IV*.[55] But, if so, the motif, adapted and developed in Shakespeare's hands, has come to serve a different end. In this play of the Prodigal Prince it is Hal who should rightly exhibit moods of repentance; and on the face of it, it seems quite illogical to transfer them to Falstaff, the tempter. Yet there are reasons why Hal could not be thus represented. In the first place, as already noted, repentance in the theological sense, repentance for sin, is not relevant to his case at all, which is rather one of a falling away from political virtues, from the duties laid upon him by his royal vocation. And in the second place, since Henry V is the ideal king of English history, Shakespeare must take great care, even in the days of his 'wildness', to guard him from the breath of scandal. As has been well observed by a recent editor: 'His riots are mere frolics. He does not get drunk and is never involved in any scandal with a woman.'[56] And there is a third reason, this time one of dramatic technique not of morals, why the repentance of the Prince must be kept in the background as much as possible, viz. that as the only satisfactory means of rounding off the two parts, it belongs especially to the last act of the play.

Yet Monsieur Remorse is a good puppet in the property-box of the old morality, and may be given excellent motions in the fingers of a skilful showman, who is laying himself out, in this play especially, to make fun of the old types. Why not shape a comic part out of it, and hand it over to Falstaff, who as the heir of traditional medieval 'antics' like the Devil, the Vice, the Fool, Riot and Lord of Misrule, may very well manage one more? Whether or not Shakespeare argued it out thus, he certainly added the ingredient of melancholy, and by so doing gave a piquancy to the sauce which immensely enhances the relish of the whole dish. If only modern actors who attempt to impersonate Falstaff would realize it !

Falstaff, then, came to stand for the repentance, as well as the riotous living, of the Prodigal Son. And striking references to the parable, four of them, seem to show that his creator was fully aware of what he was doing. 'What, will you make a younker of me? shall I not take mine ease in mine inn but I shall have my pocket picked?' [57] Sir John indignantly demands of Mistress Quickly, on discovering, or pretending to discover, the loss of his grandfather's seal-ring. The word 'younker' calls up a scene from some well-known representation of the parable, in picture or on the stage, a scene to which Shakespeare had already alluded in the following lines from *The Merchant of Venice*:

> How like a younker or a prodigal
> The scarfèd bark puts from her native bay,
> Hugged and embracèd by the strumpet wind !
> How like a prodigal doth she return,
> With over-weathered ribs and ragged sails,
> Lean, rent, and beggared by the strumpet wind ! [58]

Equally vivid is Falstaff's description of the charge of foot he led into battle at Shrewsbury as so 'dishonourable ragged' that 'you would think that I had a hundred and fifty tattered prodigals, lately come from swine-keeping, from eating draff and husks'. [59] And seeing that he calls them in the same speech 'slaves as ragged as Lazarus in the painted cloth, where the Glutton's dogs licked his sores', we may suppose that, here too, he is speaking right painted cloth, from whence he had studied his Bible [60]; an inference which seems borne out by his third reference, this time from Part II. Having, you will remember, already honoured Mistress Quickly by becoming indebted to her for a hundred marks, that is for over £65, he graciously condescends to borrow £10 more from her. And when she protests that to raise the sum she must be fain to pawn both her plate and the tapestry of her dining-chambers, he replies: 'Glasses, glasses, is the only drinking—and for thy walls, a pretty drollery or the story of the Prodigal or the German hunting in waterwork is worth a thousand of these bed-hangers and these fly-bitten tapestries.'[61] This is not just the patter of the confidence-trickster; Falstaff, we must believe, had a real liking for the Prodigal Son story, or why should that tactful person, mine Host of the Garter Inn, have gone to the trouble of having it painted, 'fresh and new', about the walls of the chamber that he let to the greasy philanderer who assumed the part of Sir John, in Windsor.[62] Not being a modern critic, the good man could not know that his guest was an impostor.

But jollification and mock-repentance do not exhaust Falstaff's roles. For most of *Henry IV* he plays the soldier, taking a hand in a couple of campaigns, the first culminating in the death of Hotspur at Shrewsbury, and the other in the encounter between Prince John and the Archbishop of York at Gaultree Forest, where the rebels are finally overthrown. In both of these he performs the useful dramatic function of supplying the light relief, and in so doing he exhibits himself as at once the supreme comic soldier of English literature and a variation of a time-worn theme, the *miles gloriosus* of Plautus. Before, however, we go to war with him, we must witness his exploits at Gad's Hill; before we consider his relation to the braggart of Roman comedy, we must address ourselves to that vexed problem: was he really a coward? And since his fate depends entirely upon the countenance of Prince Hal, there is an even earlier question to be settled: upon what terms do these two characters associate together? In a word, we must now survey the fortunes of our jolly knight as Shakespeare represents them to us, within the dramatic frame of the two parts of *Henry IV*

CHAPTER III

THE BATTLE OF GAD'S HILL

Prince Hal and Falstaff, for us merely characters in a play, were for the Elizabethans that and a great deal more. They embodied in dramatic form a miscellaneous congeries of popular notions and associations, almost all since gone out of mind, in origin quasi-historical or legendary, pagan and Christian, ethical and political, theatrical, topographical, and even gastronomic. Our review of these matters in the previous chapter, of necessity slight and perfunctory, will have served I hope to make one thing clear, namely, the kind of play Shakespeare probably intended to write about these figures, or what is much the same thing, the kind of expectations in the audience he endeavoured to satisfy.

Did he succeed? Or, if he failed, as most modern critics seem to imagine, why and where did the play miscarry? These are the questions we have now to face, and an answer to them will occupy the rest of the book. In other words, we must turn to the play itself, examine its structure, and watch the dramatist at work, in particular upon those passages which involve, directly or indirectly, the career of Falstaff, and reveal the growing alienation between him and his royal patron. Here again, the treatment must often be slight; but certain scenes and episodes demand closer scrutiny than others, either because their meaning is in doubt, or because they are crucial to the understanding of the relations between the two dramatic figures which are our principal concern. Of these none are more important than the Falstaff scenes in the first two acts of Part I, which form the theme of the present chapter.

'ENTER THE PRINCE OF WALES AND SIR JOHN FALSTAFF'

We begin with act 1, scene 2, in which both principals make their first appearance, and which must be followed carefully as it gives us the earliest glimpse we have of the relationship between them. It should open, I believe, with an empty stage, but with the sound of stertorous snöring, as of a gigantic sow, issuing from behind the curtain at the back. Enter a youth of about twenty, evidently a prince of the realm, listens a moment, then lifts the curtain and discovers an enormously fat old man asleep upon a bench. He shakes him hard; whereupon, with a huge yawn, vast chaps opening like gates upon their hinges to reveal dim caverns of throat, the sleeper slowly awakens and begins the dialogue with a drowsy 'Now Hal, what time of day is it, lad?' This setting is, of course, editorial stage-direction; that is to say, its only basis is my fancy. What is certain is that the question gives the Prince an opening for a humorous but exceedingly candid statement both of Falstaff's way of life and of his own attitude towards it. Listen:

> Thou art so fat-witted with drinking of old sack and unbuttoning thee after supper and sleeping upon benches after noon, that thou hast forgotten to demand that truly which thou wouldest truly know. What a devil hast thou to do with the time of the day? Unless hours were cups of sack, and minutes capons, and clocks the tongues of bawds, and dials the signs of leaping-houses, and the blessed sun himself a fair hot wench in flame-coloured taffeta, I see no reason why thou shouldst be so superfluous to demand the time of day.

The clock, that is to say, symbol of regularity, register of human duties, controller of the world's business, has no relevance whatever to the existence of so 'superfluous and lust-dieted' [1] a being as Falstaff. It is a devastating abstract and brief chronicle of his life, so devastating that he attempts no retort but shifts to the more entertaining ground of highway robbery, where he finds himself pressed scarcely less hard. In this first scene, at any rate, Falstaff comes off second best in his wit-combats with the Prince.

For it consists, at any rate up to the entry of Poins, largely of a set-to between them: Falstaff constantly trying to parry the Prince's thrusts by a change of subject, and the Prince as constantly twisting the talk back to Falstaff's disreputable life and what such a life leads to. It is all banter on Hal's part, and on Falstaff's the first taste we have of his peculiar blend of wit, of which as we shall see skilful evasion of the issue is a principal ingredient. Hal is easy, good-tempered, amused throughout; Falstaff, for all his familiarity and impudent sallies, is circumspect, even at times deferential. He throws out a hint about Hal's interest in a 'sweet wench', but does not venture to follow it up. He suggests that the 'heir apparent' has stretched his credit up to the limit of his expectations, and then breaks off short. And, though he condemns Hal's similes as 'unsavoury', he calls him a 'sweet young prince' immediately afterwards, while the complaint that his morals have been corrupted by Hal's company is as quickly contradicted by a second jest on his own vocation of purse-taking. Clearly everything he says is spoken with the object of entertaining his royal patron; and as clearly the entertainment is at once keenly enjoyed and taken as merely pastime. Falstaff's function, in short, as defined by this opening scene, is to act as 'the prince's jester',[2] and the Prince is not thereby in the least committed to countenance his way of living, still less to share in it. The proposal, for example, that he should take part in the highway robbery is received at first with something like indignation, even with a touch of haughtiness, and only consented to when Poins intimates, by nods and winks behind Falstaff's back, that he is planning to make a practical joke of it.

The only commentator I know to give due weight to this first Falstaff scene is John Bailey, who takes it as the key to the Prince's attitude towards him for the rest of the play. His remarks upon this attitude are worth quoting, and run as follows:

His tone throughout the scene is one of mingled affection, amusement and contempt, in which the contempt is certainly not the least conspicuous of the three. And, however much Falstaff may get the last word in wit, and he does not quite always do that, the Prince maintains throughout [the play] an ascendancy over Falstaff which is not merely one of birth and rank but one of mind and will and character.... The truth is that from first to last he is not only a prince among adventurers but a man among animals. Of these animals one has one human gift, that of speech, to a degree which has never been surpassed. But that is all....[3]

'Animal' is too modern a term, suggesting as it does a well-washed Englishman of the twentieth century catching a whiff of Falstaff's person. Elizabethans saw every day in the streets human beings too much like Falstaff, Bardolph, and the rest to class them as animals; but they would certainly think of them as a pack of scurvy rascals, inhabiting a sphere altogether remote from that to which Hal rightly belongs. With Poins matters are different. Some three or four years the Prince's senior, I take it, he is at once familiar and respectful, as a gentleman-in-waiting should be; but being also a man of birth, although a younger son,[4] he is obviously on terms with the Prince to which Falstaff, despite his knighthood, cannot aspire. Falstaff's sauciness, on the other hand, is that of 'an allowed fool';[5] and if, as I believe possible, he was first played by Will Kempe,[6] the comic man of Shakespeare's company, he would have been accepted as the 'clown' of the play directly he appeared upon the stage.

One purpose, then, of the opening Falstaff scene is exposition. As he writes it Shakespeare is pointing his audience to the end of the play, hinting at the denouement, so that they may be at ease and surrender themselves with a free conscience to all the intervening fun and riot, in the assurance that at last the Prodigal will repent—is he not beginning to repent already?—and the Tempter be brought to book. This means that Falstaff must be clearly seen for what he is, viz. an impossible companion for a king and governor, however amusing as jester to the heir apparent; and Shakespeare, accordingly, insists upon his shadier aspects, aspects which will fade into partial obscurity in the blaze of merriment that illuminates scenes to follow, but will show up distinctly again in Part II. It means also that the weakness of the hold he has upon his patron must be emphasized. This is, indeed, exhibited as a preoccupation of his mind. 'When thou art king' runs like a refrain through what he has to say, and reveals the anxieties beneath the jesting. For example, 'when thou art king, let not us that are squires of the night's body', that is to say, highwaymen, 'be called thieves', but form a special order, a recognized part of your retinue. What is to happen when the old king dies? That, as we are reminded time and again in this scene, is the leading problem of Falstaff's existence. We are to imagine it also the constant subject of his thoughts, the motive of nearly all his actions, above all the mainspring of the entertainment for the young man which he must never fail to provide, and for which we actually catch him preparing patter in Part II.[7]

And behind this problem there looms a larger and grimmer one —the gallows, the almost inevitable end of purse-takers, and high-waymen, and tall fellows who live by their wits and dissolutely spend on Tuesday morning what has been resolutely snatched on Monday night. That theme too recurs with damnable iteration in this scene. Hal introduces it; but it is too painful a subject for jest, and Falstaff swerves from it at first like a frightened horse. Yet he cannot rid his mind of it; and so after a little more skirmishing, he comes back to it with the question, 'But, I prithee, sweet wag, *shall* there be gallows standing in England when thou art king? and resolution thus fubbed as it is with the rusty curb of old father antic the law? Do not, thou, when thou art king, hang a thief!' We laugh; and the Elizabethans laughed, but in a different vein. They laughed, as they laughed at death, and pestilence, and all sorts of very unpleasant things which, being of everyday occurrence and constantly before their eyes, like scenes on the battlefield before those of the modern soldier, or bombs in the streets of London, must be laughed at to be made tolerable. To spectators for whom gibbets were nearly as common along the highway as trees, jests about the hangman were pungent enough; for those who have never seen a gibbet in their lives, except as depicted in history books, the salt has lost its savour. Yet we shall not fully understand Falstaff if we do not allow for fear of the gallows as part of his dramatic make up.

As for what is to happen when Henry of Monmouth succeeds Henry of Lancaster, the chief person concerned leaves us in no doubt on that score. For Hal also must be seen for what he is at the opening of the play. And so, when Falstaff has gone and Poins has gone, we are given in soliloquy a glimpse of his mind, the only direct view that Shakespeare vouchsafes in either part of the play.

The soliloquy seems callous and hypocritical to many modern critics. It was assuredly nothing of the kind to Shakespeare's original audience. Why not? The answer is, in the first place, that we have here a piece of dramatic convention, common in the Elizabethan theatre, but now over three hundred years out of date. The soliloquy, itself an outworn convention to us, is in this instance more than usually obsolete, since it belongs to what may be called the expository type, a type already becoming old-fashioned towards the end of the sixteenth century and seldom used again by Shakespeare after *Henry IV*. Its function was to convey information to the audience about the general drift of the play, much as a prologue did;[8] and a familiar parallel is the opening soliloquy to *Richard III*, written a few years earlier, in which Crookback confidentially informs the spectators that, though there is dissembling to be gone through first, he is 'determined to prove a villain'. In the same way Prince Hal informs us that he is determined to prove a worthy king, despite all appearances to the contrary: 'I will be good' he promises, as Victoria did on a later and different occasion. The sign-post is the more necessary in Hal's case, because two full-length performances are to intervene between promise and fulfilment. And when Part I was first staged, Part II not being yet in existence, the audience would not see the fulfilment at all. To charge him with meanness, therefore, for not communicating to Falstaff what Shakespeare makes him, for technical reasons, tell the theatre is absurd.[9] One might as well censure Richard for lack of self-control for blabbing his secrets in public.

Not that we ought, at this juncture, to be feeling that Falstaff deserves any consideration whatever—a second point, as relevant to twentieth as to sixteenth-century spectators. Modern critics invariably discuss the soliloquy in the light of their knowledge of the play as a whole, and especially of Falstaff's brilliance in the Boar's Head scene. Watch *Henry IV* in the theatre without critical prepossessions, and it will never occur to you that there is treachery to Falstaff in the soliloquy, because up to then Shakespeare has done nothing to enlist the sympathy or admiration of the audience on Falstaff's behalf. On the contrary, he has stressed the fact that he is little more than an old roué or, in Elizabethan terms, an old lad of the castle. Thus, when the Prince begins

> I know you all, and will awhile uphold
> The unyoked humour of your idleness,

it sounds inoffensive and natural enough; and when five scenes farther on the full glory of Falstaff dawns upon them, spectators do not then accuse Hal of ungenerosity, because no impression of ungenerosity was left with them as the soliloquy was uttered, while the actual terms of the soliloquy have been largely forgotten.

Yet though the soliloquy cannot be quoted in evidence against the honour and good faith of the speaker, it was intended to tell us something about his character and situation, just as Richard III's soliloquy tells us something about his. We learn that he is beginning to tire of his boon companions, beginning to look forward to the day, the inevitable day, that would dawn no one could tell when, upon which he would be called to assume the burden of kingship. We learn too that he has already made up his mind: in that day he would have to choose between Idleness and Duty, Vanity and Responsibility, and he knew which it would be. Meantime things must remain as they are. He is a banished and disgraced man,[10] but his day would come, and then he would show the world! There is a sense here of having been misjudged, a manly consciousness of his own worth in spite of appearances, perhaps even a touch of bitterness, but nothing blameworthy, unless youngmanishness be such. The Prince is beginning to grow up, that is all. Bailey, from whom I have already quoted, paraphrases the speech as follows:

> I know my friends are shaking their heads over me. They see me playing the fool and think me not capable of playing anything else. But they will one day find out their mistake. I don't mean all my days to be holidays spent among fools, however pleasant the holidays and however amusing

the fools. And when I put on my working clothes and show the wise-acres what I really am and can do, they will give me all the more credit for their surprise.[11]

And he asks, 'What is the harm of that?' Certainly, Dr Johnson could find none. 'This speech', he writes,

is very artfully introduced to keep the Prince from appearing vile [that is to say, contemptible] in the opinion of the audience; it prepares them for his future reformation, and what is yet more valuable, exhibits a natural picture of a great mind offering excuses to itself, and palliating those follies which it can neither justify nor forsake.[12]

It is a strange comment on the vagaries of criticism that a speech, which seems to one living Shakespearian 'an offence against humanity, and an offence which dramatically never becomes a skill',[13] and to another 'the most damnable piece of workmanship to be found' in Shakespeare,[14] should be praised by Johnson as a skilful expedient 'to keep the Prince from appearing vile'!

THE BELLOWING BULL-CALF

We laugh at Falstaff in act 1, scene 2, at his bland evasion of Hal's successive attacks upon his character, at his whimsical melancholy, sanctimony, and fits of repentance, at his complaints of the moral contagion of keeping company with a wicked young prince, and at the alacrity with which all this is gaily cast aside upon a mere hint of purse-taking. But it is his next appearance which provides Shakespeare with the earliest opportunity of making comic capital out of his chief visible asset: Falstaff's weight begins to tell first of all upon Gad's Hill. For there we see the 'tun of man' in action; a crescendo of action, in which both legs and lungs are more and more brought into play, and more and more surprisingly. He enters puffing and blowing, as he painfully drags himself afoot uphill, Poins having removed his horse and tied him he knows not where. Clearly, that mountain of flesh and that broken wind are incapable of further exertion. And yet, no sooner do the travellers appear than he begins shouting threats, brandishing his sword, and dancing with rage, on the fringe of the scuffle, while Bardolph, Peto and Gadshill deal with the victims. Lastly, when the robbers are in turn attacked by the men in buckram, we have him striking a hasty blow or two, turning tail, and in terror of their sword-points which prod him from behind, scurrying off as nimbly and bellowing as loudly, as ever bull-calf ran and roared at a bull-baiting. And if the varying speed at which he carries along his guts under this varying stimulus is the source of most of the comic action in the scene, reflections upon his bulk provide the theme for much of the wit. Two of Shakespeare's happiest inventions in this kind belong here: to Hal's suggestion that he should put his ear to the ground and listen for the approaching travellers Falstaff retorts, 'Have you any levers to lift me up again, being down?' and Hal adds the final touch to our vision of the fat knight in flight with the immortal words,

> Falstaff sweats to death,
> And lards the lean earth as he walks along.

Critics who tell us that Prince Henry lacks wit, forget that mighty stroke; critics who insist that Falstaff always has the best of it, ignore the fact that the fun, from beginning to end of this delicious episode, is at Falstaff's expense.

But most modern critics, as everyone knows, taking their cue from Maurice Morgann, go much farther than this: they deny that Falstaff is a coward at all. They cannot square an exhibition of genuine cowardice with 'the impression', to use Morgann's words, 'which the *whole* character of Falstaff is calculated to make on the minds of an unprejudiced audience'.[15] And though Andrew Bradley admits 'that Falstaff sometimes behaves in what we should generally call a cowardly way', he continues, 'but that does not show that he was a coward; and if the word means a person who feels painful fear in the presence of danger, and yields to that fear in spite of his better feelings and convictions, then assuredly Falstaff was no coward'.[16] What the 'better feelings and convictions' of a Falstaff may be I cannot tell, but it is unquestionable that, if we rely upon our 'impressions' of his behaviour in this scene alone, he must be pronounced an absolute coward, seeing that the audience is clearly intended to derive all possible pleasure from the agonized cries and precipitate flight of 'a person'—and such a person!—'who feels painful fear in the presence of danger, and yields to that fear'. Morgann, again, does not say what he means by 'an unprejudiced audience', but it looks very much as if he meant an audience which had never watched this scene! In any case, both Morgann and Bradley handle the scene with what may be called extreme circumspection, if not a Falstaffian discretion.

Equally weak is their treatment of the Prince's explicit comparison, two scenes later, of Falstaff's running and roaring to the terrified bellowing of a young bull baited in the ring.[17] The image is clearly intended by Shakespeare as a vivid reminder to us of the intensely amusing action upon the stage, the spectacle, that is, of this colossal old man, quivering with fright and roaring for his life, as he flies from what he takes to be pitiless assailants, though they mean him no harm beyond the tickling of his catastrophe with their swords. Had not all this happened before the eyes of the audience, the words would have been pointless. They are, as a matter of fact, little more than a repetition of words uttered by Poins immediately after Falstaff's precipitate exit on Gad's Hill. 'How the fat rogue roared!' he exclaims, as the Prince and he split their sides with laughter.[18]

Morgann, Bradley, and the rest cannot admit such conduct, because it lowers Falstaff in their esteem. How can they reconcile ignominious cowardice like this with the complete self-possession they find him displaying on all other occasions? What of that 'inexplicable touch of infinity' which Bradley in particular discovers and acclaims in him? To these questions there are two excellent answers. In the first place, the critics are, as usual, reading the play backwards. Before the Gad's Hill scene the only thing an audience knows about Falstaff is that he is an old reprobate who is at once very funny and very fat. They cannot share the reverence for him which Morgann and Bradley profess, because, unlike them, they have had no opportunity of reading both parts of the play and meditating upon them. They perceive, then, nothing at all incongruous or disturbing in the running and roaring. And if it be urged that this is only to postpone the problem, that once spectators have learnt to think of Falstaff as a butt and a coward, they can never afterwards entertain the respect and admiration which a consideration of his character as a whole shows to be his due, I counter with my second point, viz. that the critics, again as usual, are confusing stage-performance with real life. Under the conditions of theatrical illusion all sorts of things, which would seem incredible or impossible in the world of fact, may be enacted and will be accepted without question. A good actor, for example —and it may be presumed that Shakespeare, a man of the theatre, had such an actor in mind, or he would hardly have gone to the trouble of creating Falstaff—is perfectly capable of exhibiting extreme terror and complete self-possession at one and the same time.

If anyone doubts this I invite his attention to the words of that inveterate play-goer and theatre-lover, Charles Lamb, whose essay on *Stage Illusion* furnishes an illustration remarkably apt to our purpose. After speaking of the tacit understanding which a great comic player habitually establishes with his audience, he continues:

The most mortifying infirmity in human nature, to feel in ourselves, or to contemplate in another, is, perhaps, cowardice. To see a coward *done to the life* upon a stage would produce anything but mirth. Yet we most of us remember Jack Bannister's cowards. Could any thing be more agreeable, more pleasant? We loved the rogues. How was this effected but by the exquisite art of the actor in a perpetual sub-insinuation to us, the spectators, even in the extremity of the shaking fit, that he was not half such a coward as we took him for? We saw all the common symptoms of the malady upon him; the quivering lip, the cowering knees, the teeth chattering; and could have sworn 'that man was frightened'. But we forgot all the while—or kept it almost a secret to ourselves—that he never once lost his self-possession; that he let out by a thousand droll looks and gestures—meant at *us*, and not at all supposed to be visible to his fellows in the scene, that his confidence in his own resources had never once deserted him. Was this a genuine picture of a coward? or not rather a likeness, which the clever artist contrived to palm upon us instead of an original; while we secretly connived at the delusion for the purpose of greater pleasure than a more genuine counterfeiting of the imbecility, helplessness, and utter self-desertion, which we know to be concomitants of cowardice in real life, could have given us?[19]

What was within the compass of John Bannister at Drury Lane towards the end of the eighteenth century was assuredly not beyond that of Will Kempe or some other comedian on an Elizabethan stage. As I have said, the whole conception of Falstaff was probably built up in Shakespeare's mind round 'the exquisite art' of such an actor. We need not doubt then that the original impersonator of Falstaff was capable of exhibiting 'all the common symptoms of the malady' of cowardice, while he persuaded the spectators at the same time 'that he had never once lost his self-possession'.

And when Lamb exclaims 'we loved the rogues' he tells us what an audience feels, or should feel if the part is properly played, about Falstaff, as their laughter dies away with the noise of his roaring. What he leaves behind is not jeering contempt for a butt or a coward, but affection; an affection compounded of many simples: laughing sympathy for one who has 'more flesh than another man, and therefore more frailty', astonishment at the quick dexterity with which he nevertheless carries his guts away, merriment at the turning of the tables upon him, delight in the sheer absurdity of his predicament, and above all—quite illogically, though inextricably, blended with the rest—gratitude to the player for the cleverness of the whole entertainment. There is tenderness in Hal's

> Were't not for laughing, I should pity him,

a touch of admiration in Poins's

> How the fat rogue roared!

Morgann and Bradley had no need to run away from Falstaff's running away. In its proper setting, which is the theatre, that stone of stumbling is seen to be the true foundation of the affectionate mirth with which we follow his drolleries and his wit for the remainder of the play.

THE EPIC OF BUCKRAM

And if the actor who plays Falstaff can thus convince us that he is at once a coward and not a coward, still more are such spells at the call of the wizard who created him. Shakespeare, player and playwright, has suggestions of his own to palm off upon us, similar in the dramatic sphere to those conveyed by the comedian on the stage. The critics themselves lend unconscious testimony to the fact. For, just as Bannister sub-insinuated to Charles Lamb 'even in the very extremity of the shaking fit', that he was not half such a coward as he took him for, so Shakespeare persuades a large number of Falstaff's admirers that, despite the damning evidence of Gad's Hill, he is in no real sense a coward at all. In other words, he manages here, as often in other plays, to give his public the double satisfaction of eating their cake and having it still. Nor is it difficult to see how he brings it off. First of all, he amuses us with a Falstaff who is such an unmistakable coward that we can swear the man is frightened to death; then he blurs the impressions thus conveyed by plunging us into a bath of fun and wit, of impudence and self-assurance, so enchanting that the Lord of Misrule in Eastcheap almost entirely eclipses in our minds the bull-calf on Gad's Hill; next he throws out hints, a series of them, each broader than the one before, that the panic at Gad's Hill had been nothing but play-acting after all; and, lastly, he puts the old reprobate into a tight corner and shows him behaving with such coolness and resolution that we are now admiring his fortitude as unreservedly as we had formerly laughed at his cowardice. We fall a prey to these guiles the more readily that they are put upon us in the famous Boar's Head scene, which is acknowledged on all hands as without parallel in Shakespeare or elsewhere for joyous entertainment. It is to this scene we must now turn.

When we find ourselves at the tavern, our dramatic host, who well knows how to tickle the palate with kickshaws and give an edge to appetite by withholding the main dish, puts off the entry of Falstaff for a hundred lines or so. The interval is taken up with a piece of tomfoolery on the part of the Prince and Poins at the expense of Francis, the drawer. Critics have solemnly entered it up in their black book of Hal's iniquities and accused him on the strength of it of 'heartlessly endangering the poor drawer's means of subsistence'.[20] The best comment on that is Professor Kittredge's ironic reassurance: 'Sentimental readers...need not distress themselves. When Francis grew up and became an inn-keeper himself, we may be sure that he often told with intense self-satisfaction how he had once been on intimate terms with Prince Hal.'[21] Furthermore, all but Bradley of Hal's latter-day foes seem not to have noticed that he is at any rate more popular than his fat friend with the prentices in the cellar, who hail him as the very 'king of courtesy' and 'no proud Jack like Falstaff, but a Corinthian, a lad of mettle, a good boy'.[22] The point, however, would not escape Johnson, and accounts, I think, for the item, 'supercilious and haughty with common men', in his list of Fal-staff's characteristics.

But, when all is said, the main purpose of this trifling episode, apart from giving Falstaff's voice a rest after the roaring and in preparation for the strain of the scene ahead, is to keep the audience waiting, agog for him.[23] They have not seen him since the 'open and apparent shame' of Gad's Hill. What will he look like? How will he behave? Above all, by what means can he possibly elude the trap the Prince and Poins have laid? The spectators have been told something of what to expect. 'The virtue of this jest', Poins had promised, as he and his young master plot the business to-gether, 'will be the incomprehensible lies that this same fat rogue will tell us when we meet at supper, how thirty at least he fought with, what wards, what blows, what extremities he endured, and in the reproof [that is to say, disproof] of this lives the jest'.[24] There is royal sport ahead. A contemporary writer tells us that when Falstaff came on the prentice-boys stopped cracking their nuts.[25] Of all his entries none is more likely than this to have created such a sudden hush.

Yet when he appears, it is with averted head and dejected mien; it looks as if he intends after all not to show fight. To Poins's ironical 'Welcome Jack, where hast thou been?' he makes no reply, but, throwing himself wearily down at a table, first calls for sack and then breaks out into a mock-bitter speech, addressed to no one in particular, upon the villainy of cowards and the decay of manhood upon the face of the earth. Is he going to make a clean breast of it, with his talk of retiring from business, of exchanging the vocation of resolute highwayman for that of a knitter of netherstocks? Yet his harping upon cowardice and the conclusion—'There lives not three good men unhanged in England, and one of them is fat and grows old'—hardly seem in keeping with a supposition of that kind. And so, the Prince interposes sharply, 'How now, wool-sack! what mutter you?' At which the hunched figure at the table suddenly bounces into life, turns, faces them for the first time, and lets them have it:

Falstaff. A king's son! If I do not beat thee out of thy kingdom with a dagger of lath, and drive all thy subjects afore thee like a flock of wild-geese, I'll never wear hair on my face more. You, Prince of Wales!

Prince. Why, you whoreson round man! what's the matter?

Falstaff. Are you not a coward? answer me to that—and Poins there?

Thus he gets his blow in first, and accuses them of cowardice, of running away, of the very poltroonery they were about to charge him with. Of course he can show cause for it; for why had they not supported him on Gad's Hill? 'Call you that backing of your friends?' Yet how self-assured he is! May we not expect anything from impudence so unbounded?

He now launches out upon the epic of the great fight of himself and his faithful three, basely deserted by the Prince and Poins, against an ever-increasing host. Here are the 'incomprehensible lies' we had been waiting for; and the Prince winks at us, as he gravely enquires 'What, fought you with them all?' Yet is there not here something more than lies? The wink is unseen by Falstaff; but the Prince's next comment, 'Pray God, you have not murdered some of them', has a sarcasm he cannot miss. And from then onwards what the fat man says seems to take on a special meaning for us, which the Prince is not intended to perceive, and may even be too subtle for the groundlings. To him and to them everything proceeds according to plan, Poins's plan: Falstaff piles lie upon lie, and when he is at length confronted with the facts, crowns his endeavours, in a last desperate hope of escaping the toils, with the most thumping lie of the lot, the assertion that he had known the two men in buckram all along. It allows him a momentary triumph, but only of a purely verbal kind. The game is up; the braggart exposed and baffled; the success of Poins's little plot complete. Such is the purport of this famous episode on the surface.

Yet if it were indeed the whole story, might not the principal actor borrow the words of his simulacrum, the pretender to his name who is exposed and baffled at the end of *The Merry Wives of Windsor*, and ask—'Have I laid my brain in the sun and dried it, that it wants matter to prevent so gross an over-reaching as this?' That Shakespeare also has something else in view, that he intends Falstaff to establish a secret understanding with at least 'the judicious' among his audience, can I think be denied by none who give careful consideration to the dialogue. Let the reader con but one portion of it, and examine his impressions.

Prince. Pray God, you have not murdered some of them.

Falstaff. Nay, that's past praying for. I have peppered two of them. Two I am sure I have paid, two rogues in buckram suits. I tell thee what, Hal, if I tell thee a lie, spit in my face, call me horse. Thou knowest my old ward; here I lay, and there I bore my point. Four rogues in buckram let drive at me—

Hal. What, four? thou said'st but two even now.

Falstaff. Four, Hal, I told thee four.

Poins. Ay, ay, he said four.

Falstaff. These four came all afront, and mainly thrust at me. I made no more ado, but took all their seven points in my target, thus.

Prince. Seven? why, there were but four even now.

Falstaff. In buckram?

Poins. Ay, four, in buckram suits.

Falstaff. Seven, by these hilts, or I am a villain else.

Prince. Prithee, let him alone, we shall have more anon.

Falstaff. Dost thou hear me, Hal?

Prince. Ay, and mark thee too, Jack.

Falstaff. Do so, for it is worth the listening to. These nine in buckram that I told thee of—

Prince. So, two more already....

Falstaff. Began to give me ground: but I followed me close, came in hand and foot, and with a thought seven of the eleven I paid.

Prince. O monstrous! eleven buckram men grown out of two!

Falstaff. But as the devil would have it, three misbegotten knaves in Kendal green came at my back, and let drive at me, for it was so dark, Hal, that thou couldest not see thy hand.

At which point the Prince takes charge of the situation, and the show-down begins.

With Falstaff's words before us, it is hard not to agree with the American editor of the recently published Variorum text of 1 *Henry IV*, when he declares: 'It is inconceivable that he should expect to be believed as he continues this narrative.'[26] These, however, are the impressions of a reader, indeed of an editor who must in the course of his duties ponder his text much and deeply. With spectators such pondering is impossible; the traffic of the stage allows no time for careful consideration of the dialogue even by the most sharp-witted among them. Nevertheless, there the impressions are. Shakespeare is responsible for them, and the closer one examines them the stronger they grow. Test the matter by looking still closer; put the dialogue under a microscope for a moment or two.

Thus scrutinized, Falstaff's saga of Gad's Hill falls into two clearly marked sections: fytte one dealing with the battle in general, and fytte two concerned with the buckram men alone. And the switch from the one to the other is surprising, even a trifle forced.

A minute earlier he had been speaking of 'two or three and fifty upon poor old Jack'. Why this sudden singling out of 'two rogues in buckram suits', if not to inform us that he knows, well enough, who they were? Surely, it is his turn to wink at the audience now. Moreover, the exaggerations in the fytte of the buckram men are of a quite different order from the rest. Hitherto the number of enemies had increased, with great rapidity indeed, but not impossibly after a haphazard, almost natural, fashion; now it mounts in a regular series, in a kind of arithmetical progression, two, four, seven, nine, eleven, while the passage from one number to the next is made without pause of any kind.[27] To what purpose is all this if it be not to attract our attention and convince us that the whole business is a joke? Note too the engaging air of innocence with which he meets the running challenge of the Prince and Poins: the sadly protesting 'Four, Hal, I told thee four', the blandly puzzled query[28] 'In buckram?' and the indignant outburst 'Seven, by these hilts, or I am a villain else'. Finally, there is the identification of the misbegotten knaves in Kendal green on a pitch-black night, which is like a simple catch, deliberately played straight into the opponents' hands, so as to bring the innings to an end.[29] And if all this is patent enough, as we pore over the pages of 1 *Henry IV*, might it not be brought out in the theatre when Falstaff is played by a comedian capable of revealing Shakespeare's intentions, to quote Lamb once more, by 'looks and gestures—meant at us, and not at all supposed to be visible to his fellows in the scene'?

Surely it might, if only gradually, and perhaps not to all parts of the audience. In short, the solution I offer to a well-worn critical problem is that Shakespeare filled his dialogue with these gathering hints in order to produce an ever-deepening impression upon the brighter spirits in the theatre. Having riveted their attention from the outset by Falstaff's air of self-assurance and the impudent attempt to transfer the charge of cowardice to the Prince and Poins, he drives them step by step first to a suspicion and then to a belief that the old scoundrel very well knows what he is about and that he holds the trump card in his hand, while letting his opponents imagine that they are playing their own little game. In the rapid give and take of spoken dialogue, listeners have little time to consider the points individually, and some points will appeal more to one type of intelligence, others to another; but, as the hints grow broader and more numerous, they prove, at last and in the aggregate, overwhelming. Thus, when the climax comes, alert minds are ready to take Falstaff's word for it that he had recognized the men in buckram from the beginning, and are almost prepared to doubt their own eyes and ears which had seen and heard the running and the roaring on Gad's Hill.

But at this point I can overhear some absolute knave protesting, 'All very ingenious, no doubt'—'ingenious' would be the word—'but was Falstaff a coward or not? what *really* happened at Gad's Hill?' To which I can only reply: nothing ever 'really happens' on the stage; and suggest that Shakespeare deliberately left the question of Falstaff's cowardice as a problem to be debated by the inns-of-court men of his audience in the taverns of Shoreditch after the play was over. And if he chanced himself to be present, with other members of the company, and was appealed to on the matter, I fancy he might respond, with a glance and a smile at Heminge, the business manager, 'Come again, gentlemen, to-morrow afternoon, and you will see'. The world has been coming again and again ever since—and the debate continues.

In that debate there is one matter which I do not think has yet been clearly brought out and, remaining obscure, has tended to confuse the issue. It cannot be emphasized too much that the understanding which, I contend, Falstaff establishes with members of the audience is a secret one, and not at all intended for the Prince and Poins. Logically, no doubt, the various points made above should be as obvious to them as to judicious spectators. But we are moving in theatreland, not in the realm of logic; and at the theatre, as every theatre-goer knows, actions and meanings which are plain as a pikestaff to the whole auditorium often appear to pass entirely unnoticed by some or all of the other characters on the stage, more especially when the players concerned deliberately act such blindness. And that Shakespeare meant the Prince and Poins to be thus blind is proved by their asides to each other as the tale of the buckram men grows: 'Prithee, let him alone; we shall have more anon', and 'So, two more already!' and again 'O monstrous; eleven buckram men grown out of two!' They are in a plot together, the plot laid in the second scene of the play. And though the lies are still more extravagant, and the jest proportionately richer, than Poins could have dared to hope, it is the *kind* of jest he had promised, a feast of braggadocio, nothing else. Of Falstaff's secret intelligence with the audience, the special tit-bit of comic aside, they know nothing; for as he laughs at them behind his hand, they are busy laughing together, at him.

'And in the reproof of this lives the jest' had been the crown of Poins's forecast; and the 'reproof' once again more than answers all expectations, when it comes to the point; once again carries with it its second meaning for the audience. Before Mistress Quickly's fire, or what represented it on Shakespeare's stage, there should, I think, be a high-backed wooden settle. Upon this, out of breath with his catalogue of base comparisons, Falstaff collapses, and so remains hidden from the audience, while the Prince and Poins, standing at either end of the settle and so concealing him still further, overwhelm him with their plain tale of what took place at the battle of Gad's Hill. 'What trick', Hal concludes, 'what device, what starting-hole, canst thou now find out to hide thee from this open and apparent shame?' To which Poins adds, 'Come, let's hear Jack—what trick hast thou now?' They think— they *know*—that they have him at last. But even as Poins is speaking a great red face rises, sun-like, above the back of the settle; a smile of triumph steals across it; and then, with solemn emphasis, there comes the consummate retort:[30]

By the Lord, I knew ye as well as he that made ye! Why, hear you, my masters, was it for me to kill the heir-apparent? should I turn upon the true prince? why, thou knowest I am as valiant as Hercules: but beware instinct—the lion will not touch the true prince. Instinct is a great matter—I was now a coward upon instinct. I shall think the better of myself and thee during my life; I for a valiant lion, and thou for a true prince.

Talking to Boswell one day about Samuel Foote, the famous comic actor and improvisatore of his age, Dr Johnson remarked: 'One species of wit he has in an eminent degree, that of escape. You drive him into a corner with both hands; but he's gone, Sir, when you are thinking you have got him—like an animal that jumps over your head.'[31] This exactly describes the kind of wit in which Falstaff excelled, and the game which the Prince and Poins play time and again with him. The quarry always succeeds in evading them; but never does he put his escape-wit to more adroit use than on this occasion. To them the crowning lie is completely unexpected and quite unanswerable. To many readers and to the less barren of spectators it affords an even greater entertainment, that of being, as they have now come to believe, nothing but the simple truth!

'I DENY YOUR MAJOR'

No impressions received from the rest of the scene will disturb this faith. Certainly not Falstaff's cry for mercy, 'Ah, no more of that, Hal, an thou lovest me', when the Prince proposes his running away as the argument for an extempore play, or the Prince's sly allusions to instinct a little later on. For it is part of the game to admit, when all is over, that the trick, device, or starting-hole is nothing more. The Prince must have his jest, and the jester fall in with it, humouring him with his apparent triumph. And then comes in the sweetest morsel of the night, the mock-interviews between the Prince of Wales and his father, Falstaff and Hal taking the parts, turn and turn about. We must hence, and leave it un-picked, alas, because—blessed scene—it raises no problems that need disentangling. Only this is to be noted: that here, if anywhere in the play, Falstaff is to be seen, as Bradley has it, 'in bliss'; that it is beyond doubt the serene happiness and unparalleled intellectual brilliance he now displays which have gained him his august station in the mythology of modern man; and that all this serves still further to obliterate from our minds the memory of his earlier fit of abject terror. Yet it is ever Shakespeare's way to thrust his bolts well home. Accordingly, towards the end of the scene, he makes Hal directly charge Falstaff with being a coward by nature, only in order to give him the opportunity first of denying it absolutely and then of attesting the truth of his denial by action. Let me remind you of the circumstances.

The merriment of the play extempore is rudely interrupted by a thundering at the tavern gate:

Enter Bardolph, running

Bardolph. O, my lord, my lord, the sheriff with a most monstrous watch is at the door!

Falstaff. Out ye rogue! play out the play. I have much to say in the behalf of that Falstaff.

Enter the Hostess

Hostess. O Jesu, my lord, my lord!—

Prince. Heigh, heigh! the devil rides upon a fiddlestick. What's the matter?

Hostess. The sheriff and all the watch are at the door, they are come to search the house, shall I let them in?

There is a question, indeed! If she does, Falstaff will inevitably be captured. A summary examination by the Sheriff, a journey through jeering crowds to Tyburn in the hangman's cart, the noosing of the halter about his neck, the climb up the ladder, the final leap from the ridge of the gallows: all are before him at that moment, the haunting fears he dreads most.[32] For there is no possibility of escape: no shamming dead as on the battlefield, no running away as at Gad's Hill. Disguise is out of the question; the gross fat man is known as well as Paul's. He is trapped—trapped like a rat. His only hope is that the Prince will use his royal authority to refuse admittance to the officers of the law; and he cannot be sure of the Prince. Does he fall upon his knees and beg his 'sweet honey lord' to save him somehow, anyhow? Sir John of Windsor might, not this Falstaff. He goes on with the play as if there were no sheriffs in life. Yet as he continues to speak 'in the behalf of that Falstaff', what he says, in jest, shows clearly enough that he realizes to the full the predicament he is in. 'Shall I let them in?' demands Mistress Quickly.

Falstaff. Dost thou hear, Hal? never call a true piece of gold a counterfeit. Thou art essentially mad, without seeming so.

—in other words, 'Don't let me down by calling a true-mettled fellow a false thief. Appearances are deceptive; you, for example, are really mad, though you don't look it.'

Prince. And thou a natural coward, without instinct.
Falstaff. I deny your major. If you will deny the sheriff, so, if not, let him enter. If I become not a cart as well as another man, a plague upon my bringing up! I hope I shall be as soon strangled with a halter as another.

It is a magnificent display of stoutness of heart, which looks Death straight in the eyes without blinking or turning aside.[33] And it succeeds, if Hal's resolution really needs stiffening. For, though he does not 'deny the sheriff', he finds a better way by hiding the hunted man behind the arras. And once Falstaff, from that covert, hears the suave declaration,

> The man, I do assure you, is not here,

he knows that all is well, and—the strain relaxed—falls fast asleep. He has disproved the Prince's major, and though he never fights longer than he sees reason, or fights at all if he can avoid it, we hear no more of his 'cowardice' for the rest of the play.[34]

That he should sleep so calmly is itself the final answer to the Prince's slanderous story of the events on Gad's Hill, and to our own receding impressions: the two Falstaffs cannot be the same man. The sleep also adds the crowning touch of fun to the greatest of comic scenes; or so I fancy. For, as the Prince stands parleying with the Sheriff and his witness, the carrier, a strange sound steals upon their ears, and is soon audible even to the remotest corners of the theatre. The spectators recognize it at once, since they have heard it before; being nothing else than the trumpet-snore that preceded Falstaff's first entry. To Master Sheriff, however, it is a new and interesting noise; he looks about and above him; and then turns to the Prince with an air of perplexity. Hal, for his part, is on tenterhooks; and gets rid of the pair of them with all possible despatch.

There follows the searching of his pockets by Poins, the discovery of the brief but revealing supper-bill, and the hurried departure of the Prince and Poins for the wars. Through all this Falstaff sleeps on, and is left to sleep till day. He had earned his rest. The pace of this business, from the moment when Poins robs him of his horse on Gad's Hill until the Sheriff runs him to ground, had been terrific. What it cost him in the sweat of his brow, to say nothing of lard from the rest of his person, may be gathered from words he speaks to Bardolph on the following day.

Am I not fallen away vilely since this last action? do I not bate? do I not dwindle? Why, my skin hangs about me like an old lady's loose gown, I am withered like an old apple-john.

CHAPTER IV

THE PRINCE GROWS UP

In the last chapter we were obliged to discuss minutiae and scrutinize the text closely in order to remove a stone of stumbling lying across the very threshold of the play. In the chapter that follows this one we shall be able to stand back somewhat and trace the fortunes of the fat knight in more general terms, from his departure for Shrewsbury until he is seen waiting, with Justice Shallow, at the doors of Westminster Abbey to salute his 'sweet boy' as King of England: at which juncture, as we had been warned from the first, the blind goddess turns her wheel, and our Humpty-dumpty comes toppling to the ground. But the cause of this catastrophe is the withdrawal of the newly anointed king's favour, and something, however inadequate, must now be said about the quality and development of that young man's character.

THE TRUANT'S RETURN TO CHIVALRY

In *Henry IV* Shakespeare handles, among other human relationships, the disharmony that often arises between parent and child as the latter begins to grow up. It is a difficult time in any walk of life; but strained relations between a reigning sovereign, of either sex, and the heir to the throne seem almost to partake of the order of nature. Within living memory there have been two examples at Windsor, while the story of Wilhelm II of Germany and his mother shows that it is not necessarily a product of the English climate. Individual instances are, of course, attended by special circumstances, and the attitude of Henry IV towards his son was to some extent the result of the peculiar conditions of his own accession. He had usurped the throne from Richard II, whom he subsequently murdered; he was not even Richard's heir, Mortimer his cousin being next in lineal succession. Thus his reign and all his actions are overhung with the consciousness both of personal guilt and of insecurity of tenure, a fact that Shakespeare never misses an opportunity of underlining. 'Uneasy lies the head that usurps a crown' might be taken as the motto of what Johnson calls the 'tragical part' of the play, and the worry of it, combined with ill-health, finally wears the King out. As one of his sons says,

> Th'incessant care and labour of his mind
> Hath wrought the mure that should confine it in
> So thin that life looks through and will break out.[1]

Whatever Bolingbroke may be in *Richard II*, King Henry IV is no hard crafty politician but a man sick in body and spirit, a pathetic figure. In the hope of purging his soul of the crimes that gained him his throne, he dreams of a crusade; and Heaven's anger at those crimes seems to him most evident in the strange, disastrous behaviour of his heir. He misunderstands his son, of course, misunderstands him completely; but it is the nature of fathers to misunderstand their sons.

As for the son himself, Princes of Wales have so often in youth chosen to break away from court formalities and live at freedom with boon companions of their own choosing, that we might take Prince Hal's situation as the almost inevitable consequence of his position in life. There are special points, however, about his situation too which should not be overlooked. At the opening of the play, for instance, the quarrel had been going on for some time. He speaks, at the first interview with his father, of

> The long grown wounds of my intemperature;[2]

and at least twelve months before, at the end of *Richard II*, we have Bolingbroke referring to the wild courses of his 'young, wanton and effeminate boy'. Hal is historically little more than sixteen years old at the battle of Shrewsbury, and though he seems twenty at least in Shakespeare, he must have been very young when first, under the guidance of Poins we may surmise, he became 'an Ephesian of the old church' and got to know Falstaff at the Boar's Head; a point to be borne in mind in our judgement of him. His conduct, again, has not only brought him into public contempt, as is proved by Hotspur's references in the third scene, but has led to the loss of his seat at the Privy Council and his banishment from the court, as the King informs us at the first interview.[3] Thus the breach between father and son is not only of long standing but has gone deep. On the other hand, we learn from the Prince's soliloquy already dealt with that he is now tiring of his unchartered freedom, and looking forward vaguely to the day when he will resume the responsibilities of his station. In a word, he is ceasing to be a boy. As the play goes forward, we are in fact to watch him growing up and becoming a man, and a man, do not let us forget, who represents the ideal king, whether leader or governor, in Elizabethan eyes.

One more point, a technical point, should be brought out in this connection. Critics complain that Hal's character is 'not the offspring of the poet's reflection and passion'.[4] Does this amount to anything more than a statement that he is not so self-revealing as Hamlet, or Macbeth or Richard II or even Harry Hotspur? The kind of reserve that springs from absence of self-regard is, in point of fact, one of his principal characteristics; and such a feature is difficult to represent in dialogue. Everything depends upon bearing, expression of countenance, silences, just those things which can hardly, if at all, be conveyed in a book. All that remains of Shakespeare is his book; his directions to the players are gone beyond recall. We have, therefore, no means of telling just how he wished Hal to be played. But we have equally no right to assume that Hal is heartless, because he does not, like Richard II, wear his heart upon his sleeve. He is just not interested in Hal and so does not talk about him, except banteringly in the Falstaff scenes. And there is more than natural reserve to be reckoned with. By the very nature of his material Shakespeare was restricted in his opportunities of exhibiting the Prince's character. While he is in disgrace, and his creator is obliged to keep him more or less thus eclipsed until the death of his father, Hal can only be shown in speech with his boon companions, and in an occasional interview with the King. Why not, it may be said, give him his Horatio like

Hamlet? The answer is that Shakespeare does so; he gives him Poins, and the discovery of the worthlessness of this friend is the subject of one of the most moving and revealing scenes in which the Prince figures.[5] In view of all this, to assert, as Bradley does, that Hal is incapable of tenderness or affection except towards members of his own family,[6] is surely a quite unwarranted assumption. We shall find it directly contradicted by dramatic facts which emerge at a later stage. For the present we have to rest content with what we may glean from the talk he has with his father, but we need feel under no necessity of discounting what he then says and does as prompted solely by family ties or dynastic policy.

The insurrection of the Percies obliges the King to summon the Prince of Wales, that he may find out exactly where he stands and if he can be made use of in this crisis which threatens the newly established dynasty; and we are prepared for an interview, by Sir John Bracy's summons, which interrupts the jollification at the Boar's Head, and by Falstaff and Hal themselves, who rehearse the scene in comic anticipation.[7] His Majesty begins with bitter chiding, as Falstaff had prophesied he would. He hints at the affair with the Lord Chief Justice (to which Shakespeare makes no direct reference before Part II), and speaks of the lost seat at the Council and the banishment from court. But the burden of his charge is that Harry has made himself cheap in the eyes of men, which is the very last thing the representative of a family with a doubtful title to the throne should permit himself. He compares him with the reckless, feckless, Richard II—Henry can never stop thinking about Richard—who had also come to grief through making himself cheap, while he likens Hotspur, stealing away men's hearts by prowess and policy, to himself before he pushed Richard from his stool. Finally he turns upon his son, calls him his 'nearest, dearest enemy', and concludes with an outburst declaring him

> like enough through vassal fear,
> Base inclination and the start of spleen,
> To fight against me under Percy's pay.

From beginning to end of the interview the Prince's attitude is perfect, as it ever is with his father. He accepts the blame as in part deserved, though protesting that his scrapes have been grossly exaggerated by 'smiling pickthanks and base newsmongers'. He promises with a noble and touching simplicity, in which dignity mingles with humility,

> I shall hereafter, my thrice gracious lord,
> Be more myself.

But the King's last bitter taunt stings him in self-defence to proclaim more positive intentions; he will reinstate himself in the eyes of his father (it is characteristic that he speaks and thinks of no rehabilitation of a more public kind) by meeting Hotspur on the battlefield and wresting the crown of chivalry from his brow. The King, convinced by the fervour of the protest, restores him to his favour and confidence, and even associates him in the command of the army of the west. Thus the feet of the Prince are definitely set upon the path of reformation. The rebellion has brought him an earlier opportunity than he hoped of

> breaking through the foul and ugly mists
> Of vapours that did seem to strangle him.

Yet the process is not to be carried out in a day. It is, in fact, a double process, comprising two distinct stages. As a 'truant to chivalry'[8] he has first to prove himself a soldier and a leader; and this he accomplishes on the field of Shrewsbury. It is only later that the companion of Riot has a chance of displaying the qualities, or acknowledging the loyalties, of the governor. Viewing *Henry IV* as a whole, we may label Part I the Return to Chivalry; Part II the Atonement with Justice.

Shakespeare cannot bring horsemen upon the stage, but he depicts his young knight for us in the words of Sir Richard Vernon, who bears news to the rebel camp of the approach of the King's forces towards Shrewsbury. 'Where' Hotspur contemptuously asks him,

> Where is his son,
> The nimble-footed madcap Prince of Wales,
> And his comrades, that daff the world aside,
> And bid it pass?

To which Vernon replies:

> All furnished, all in arms;
> All plumed like estridges that wing the wind,
> Baited like eagles having lately bathed,
> Glittering in golden coats like images,
> As full of spirit as the month of May,
> And gorgeous as the sun at midsummer;
> Wanton as youthful goats, wild as young bulls.
> I saw young Harry with his beaver on,
> His cuisses on his thighs, gallantly armed,
> Rise from the ground like feathered Mercury,
> And vaulted with such ease into his seat,
> As if an angel dropped down from the clouds,
> To turn and wind a fiery Pegasus,
> And witch the world with noble horsemanship.[9]

'A more lively representation', comments Dr Johnson, 'of young men ardent for enterprize, perhaps no writer has ever given.' And that Shakespeare in penning these lines, turned for inspiration to Spenser's description of the Red Cross Knight rising lusty as an eagle from the Well of Life shows (i) that he desired to call up a vision of chivalry in its perfection, and (ii) that in evoking this vision he had specially in mind the notion of regeneration.

It is Vernon again who tells us that the Prince has a knightly bearing and action in keeping with his appearance as a warrior. Speaking of the challenge which he and Worcester are commissioned by the Prince to convey to Hotspur, he declares:

> I never in my life
> Did hear a challenge urged more modestly,
> Unless a brother should a brother dare
> To gentle exercise and proof of arms.[10]

And he goes on to stress, in glowing terms, a generosity of spirit towards his rival and a humble-mindedness when speaking of himself, which reminds us, on the one hand, of Hamlet's courtesy to Laertes before the duel and, on the other, of the attitude of Malory's Lancelot towards his fellow-knights.

In the battle scenes themselves, Shakespeare bends all his energy to enhance the honour of his hero, even departing from the chroniclers to do so. The conspicuous part he plays is exhibited in marked contrast to that of the King. The King, for example, dresses many men in his coats so as to shield himself: the wounded Hal refuses to withdraw to his tent, yet is all the while glowing with pride at his younger brother's prowess. Holinshed, again, says nothing of the Prince coming to his father's rescue, when sore beset by the terrible Douglas; but Shakespeare borrows this significant detail from the poet Daniel and elaborates it. Indeed, throughout the battle we are made to feel that the Prince is the real leader and inspirer of the royal army, a role which Holinshed ascribes to the King. There follows the encounter and fight with Hotspur, also taken from Daniel, which would be realistically played on the Elizabethan stage, and the tender, almost brotherly, speech which he utters over his slain foe. This last is Shakespeare's alone. Furthermore, Shakespeare gives the gentle victor an action to match his words worthy of the occasion in a supreme degree; an action the recovery of which I owe to an American scholar.[11]

> But let my favours hide thy mangled face,

says the Prince bending forward to cover those staring eyes,

> And even in thy behalf I'll thank myself
> For doing these fair rites of tenderness.[12]

The thought, all the more charming for its boyishness, is prompted by a rush of generous emotion. But what are these favours, these rites of tenderness? The fight over, the Prince has removed his beaver and holds it in his hand. The 'favours' it bears are Prince of Wales's feathers, one or two of which he now reverently lays across the face of his mighty enemy. It is a gesture worthy of Sir Philip Sidney himself; the crowning touch in the vision

Shakespeare gives us of his paladin Prince, brave as a lion, tender as a woman.

As he turns from the body of Hotspur, Hal sees a vaster corpse nearby, and is moved to utter another epitaph in a different key.

> What! old acquaintance! could not all this flesh
> Keep in a little life? poor Jack, farewell!
> I could have better spared a better man:
> O, I should have a heavy miss of thee,
> If I were much in love with vanity!

There is genuine sorrow here; Falstaff had given him too much pleasure and amusement for him to face his death without a pang. But the tone, which may be compared with Hamlet's when confronted with Yorick's skull, is that of a prince speaking of his dead jester, not of friend taking leave of familiar friend; and what there is of affection is mainly retrospective. In the new world that opens up at Shrewsbury there is little place left for the follies of the past.

> O, I should have a heavy miss of thee,
> If I were much in love with vanity.

It is Hal's real farewell to the old life; and after Shrewsbury Falstaff is never again on the same terms with his patron.

The two epitaphs are deliberately placed side by side. Can there be any reasonable doubt which seemed to Shakespeare the more important? The overthrow of Hotspur is the turning point not only of the political plot of the two Parts but also in the development of the Prince's character. The son has fulfilled the promises made to his father; the heir has freed the monarchy of its deadliest foe; the youth has proved, to himself, that he need fear no rival in Britain as soldier and general. Yet these are not the considerations first in his mind; for himself and his own affairs are never uppermost in the consciousness of this character. The epitaph on Hotspur contains not a word of triumph; its theme is the greatness of the slain man's spirit, the tragedy of his fall, and what may be done to reverence him in death. With such solemn thoughts does Shakespeare's hero turn to Falstaff. Is it surprising that he should be out of love with Vanity at a moment like this? The point is of interest technically, since the moment balances and adumbrates a still more solemn moment at the end of Part II in which he also encounters Falstaff and has by then come to be even less in love with what he represents.

How little the sense of personal triumph enters into what he feels about the overthrow of Hotspur is shown by his willingness to surrender all claims when his 'old acquaintance' surprisingly comes to life again and asserts that the honour belongs to him.

> For my part, if a lie may do thee grace,
> I'll gild it with the happiest terms I have,

is his good-humoured aside. It is in keeping with the easy amiability which first took him to the Boar's Head and made him popular with the drawers when he got there. But it is also an instance of selflessness and generosity which appears to have been as much overlooked by critics as have its effects upon the character of Falstaff in Part II.[13] For the Prince keeps his promise, and it will be noticed that the King shows no consciousness in the next scene of Part I, which is the last, that his son has had any share in the slaying of his chief enemy.

All that Shakespeare does for the Prince in this scene, which might so easily have been converted into one of public triumph and applause on his behalf, is to offer yet another example of his native magnanimity. Douglas, a captured fugitive, lies bruised at his tent and in his power. He desires the King to grant him the disposal of this great soldier; and when consent is given he turns to the brother who had just fleshed his maiden sword and bids him deliver the captive

> Up to his pleasure, ransomless and free,

inasmuch as

> His valour shown upon our crests to-day
> Hath taught us how to cherish such high deeds,
> Even in the bosom of our adversaries.

The 'high courtesy' of this act, which would seem of the very essence of chivalry to Elizabethans and can still win our admiration in an age of tanks and bombs, could only have occurred to a spirit of real nobility. That the same spirit should then bestow upon another the delight of its execution more than doubles the quality of its gallantry. Sir Lancelot himself could not have been more courteous, more self-effacing.

Shakespeare inherited from chroniclers a sudden conversion for Prince Hal of an almost miraculous kind. This he is at pains to make reasonable and human, and he does so by marking it off, as I have said, into various stages, thereby accustoming the audience more and more to the notion of it and giving an impression of gradual development of character, the development of a kind normal in the passage from adolescence to manhood. There is so much else to be done in the play, that he cannot, as in *Hamlet*, keep the young man constantly beneath the limelight of our attention; he has scope for intermittent glimpses only. But these glimpses are given us at the right moments, and are fully sufficient for the purpose, if we are following the play with the attention a dramatist may legitimately expect; an expectation thwarted unfortunately in the present instance by the fact that the play is never seen as a whole upon the modern stage and that the intense preoccupation of the romantic critics with the character of Falstaff has thrown a shadow of obscurity over all the scenes and characters in which he is not directly concerned. In Part I we are afforded three opportunities of seeing the mind of the Prince, in each of which he appears more conscious than before of the obligations of his vocation: (i) the soliloquy after his first scene with Falstaff in which he is shown growing tired of tavern life and trying, in a rather boyish fashion, to palliate, as Johnson says, 'those follies which he can neither justify nor forsake'; (ii) the interview with his father, in which, awakened for the first time to the full significance of his position by the appalling suspicions of disloyalty which the King entertains, he takes a solemn vow to meet Hotspur in the field and either rob him of his title as the flower of chivalry or perish in the attempt; and (iii) the battle of Shrewsbury, the climax of Part I, in which for some six scenes he is brought continuously before us, either in person or through the report of other characters, so that we see more of him than we have ever seen before, and discover him to be not only a general who can win a battle and a soldier who can beat to the ground the best swordsman in the country, not only the soul of courtesy, whose chief thought is respect for the defeated and tenderness for the fallen, but a man so large-hearted and unmindful of self that, having wrested the laurels of the age from Hotspur's brow, he loses interest in the garland itself, is only amused when Falstaff, finding it lying in his way, sets it on his own head, and promises to aid and abet the fraud, as a favour to a friend and a jest to himself.

HONOUR: THE SCUTCHEON AND THE SPIRIT

Hal's acquiescence in Falstaff's false claim to Hotspur's overthrow is connected with the attitude of all three men towards Honour, which has not, I think, been rightly understood. To Hotspur, whom the King describes as the 'child of honour and renown'[14] and Douglas as 'king of honour',[15] Honour is a divinity; he grows ecstatic at the thought; he talks of leaping to the moon or diving to the bottom of the sea to find his goddess. But he will take her on one condition only: that he

> might wear
> *Without corrival* all her dignities.[16]

The glory to be shared with others is not worth having. In a word, the honour of which he dreams is personal renown and nothing else; a conception which, for all its implications of bravery in battle and contempt for danger and death, is a purely selfish one. The famous soliloquy on Honour shows that Falstaff also puts this meaning upon it, while at the same time declaring that the game is not worth the candle. For what is this renown, this 'bubble reputation' as Shakespeare calls it elsewhere, when one examines it? A word, useless to the dead, and short-lived to the living, since there will always be backbiters to belittle it. At best, it is 'a mere

scutcheon', a cheap piece of painted hatchment to grace a man's
funeral. Yet, though he scornfully refuses to risk life and limb in
playing for such a hazard, he is as willing as anyone else to make
capital out of it when he finds it in his way by chance; and it is not
an accident that Shakespeare shows this contemner of 'honour'
bearing off the highest honours of the field. For grant Hotspur's
assumptions, which were no doubt those of most Elizabethan
gentlemen, and Falstaff's catechism is unanswerable, and his luck
an illustration of its truth. Nor does the honour that comes to him
without risk do him any good in the end, as the sequel proves.
Morgann calls Falstaff a 'military free-thinker': military cynic
would have been a better term. In his catechism he is as usual the
'old soldier', bringing everything to the touch of self-interest.
And behind the soliloquy, and the fraudulent claim that follows,
may be detected Shakespeare's own comment upon Hotspur. This
personal glory, for which Percy gives his life, distracts the realm
with civil war, and is willing to carve it up into three separate
kingdoms, is an illusion; its only object is self-interest, and yet the
self—as even this rascally old camp-follower can see—has nothing
to gain from it. Certainly, Hotspur gains nothing; his corpse lies
bleeding and grinning on the ground, to be dishonourably stabbed
by the same old scoundrel, who hoists it on his back and pitches
it about like so much luggage. As for renown, what chance
has a defeated rebel of that?

Harry Monmouth too has his speeches upon Honour: the speech
at the first meeting with his father, in which he vows by over-
throwing Hotspur to wipe out the *dis*honour the King attributes
to him; and the speech on St Crispin's Eve (if I may for a moment
contravene my own canons and look forward into the next play)
when as commander-in-chief he leads the little English host against
overwhelming odds on the field of Agincourt. In the first he
promises

> That I shall make this northern youth exchange
> His glorious deeds for my indignities.
> Percy is but my factor, good my lord,

> To engross up glorious deeds on my behalf,
> And I will call him to so strict account
> That he shall render every glory up,
> Yea, even the slightest worship of his time,
> Or I will tear the reckoning from his heart.

And in the second he declares that

> if it be a sin to covet honour
> I am the most offending soul alive.[17]

Both sound at first like Hotspur's sentiments, and many critics have failed to detect the difference. Yet when he speaks of robbing Percy of his glory, he is thinking, not of personal reputation, but of regaining his father's good opinion, while his conduct at Shrewsbury shows him coveting, not the renown of glorious deeds, but the deeds themselves: once having set himself right with his conscience, he unconcernedly passes on the credit to another. And we have only to glance at the speech before Agincourt to see that the honour he then covets is for his army, not himself. So far is he from deeming his fellow-soldiers rivals, he calls them brothers:

> And Crispin Crispian shall ne'er go by,
> From this day to the ending of the world,
> But we in it shall be remembered,
> We few, we happy few, we band of brothers;
> For he to-day that sheds his blood with me
> Shall be my brother.[18]

Thus the Prince, who is to figure in the sequel to *Henry IV* as 'the mirror of all Christian kings', is already at Shrewsbury the soul of true honour, caring nothing for renown, for the outward show of honour in the eyes of men, so long as he has proved himself worthy of its inner substance in his own. And this substance is only personal in so far as every patriot may share in it; for the honour he covets is to add to the honour of England. It is a conception peculiar to himself. The old King has not a notion of it, or he could never have called Hotspur 'the child of honour', have compared himself arriving at Ravenspurgh with Hotspur, or think of the crown he has usurped as a purely personal possession. In earlier plays, the ardently patriotic speeches of the Bastard and of the dying Gaunt come near to it, but are not related expressly to military deeds. It would be interesting to enquire how far it was also new to Shakespeare.[19]

THE RECONCILIATION BETWEEN FATHER AND SON

Before we consider in detail what the Prince does in Part II, it will be well to give a brief summary of the events in which he is engaged between the death of Hotspur and his second interview with his father. At the end of Part I, having crushed the main army of the rebels at Shrewsbury, the King divides his forces, bidding Prince John and Westmoreland proceed with their 'dearest speed' to attack Northumberland and Archbishop Scroop in Yorkshire, while he and the Prince of Wales move towards the Principality to deal with Glendower and the Earl of March. Shakespeare uses time like elastic, to be stretched at will; so that, if we narrowly examine the chronology of events at the beginning of Part II, as we are not of course intended to do, we find ourselves in Northumberland only a few days after Shrewsbury, and immediately after that in London when, if we reckon by the events in Wales, it must be several weeks, if not months, later. In these London scenes, indeed, the Welsh expedition is already over, and the Prince, together with his father, now very ill, are on their way home, at Basingstoke, whence they reach Westminster on the following day. In the scene with Poins, to be presently examined, which gives us the earliest appearance of the Prince in Part II, he has evidently just arrived from Wales and is dead tired after the journey. He seeks diversion by adjourning that same evening to the Boar's Head, where disguised as a drawer he spies upon Falstaff with Doll and overhears the abuse of himself. The fun that follows is interrupted by Peto, who brings news of the impending clash between the armies in Yorkshire and of the search by a dozen sweating captains for the laggard Falstaff. Whereupon the Prince, ashamed of himself for playing the fool at such a time, seizes sword and cloak and hurries away.

What he is doing between that moment and the scene at the King's death-bed, where we next see him, we are not informed. All we know is that the interval is long enough for Falstaff to travel from London to Gaultree Forest, arriving conveniently late for the main battle, if battle it can be called, and for Prince John to travel back with news of his treacherous victory over the rebels, reaching Westminster just in time to see his father alive. In the first of the two scenes before his death, the King asks anxiously after the Prince of Wales, and is told by one brother that he is hunting at Windsor and by another that he is dining 'with Poins and other his continual followers'; which leaves us to infer that, with his father lying sick at court and with nothing to occupy his own energies, the young man is naturally enough spending his time amusing himself as best he can. But the point is only made to give occasion for the King's outburst against him in the next scene, and is quickly forgotten in the Prince's noble speech in reply. The truth is that after Shrewsbury, that is for most of Part II, Shakespeare deliberately keeps his Prince in the background for technical reasons. He does no more fighting; and the chief figure in the rounding up of the northern rebels, to which five scenes are devoted, is not Westmoreland, as in Holinshed, but Prince John, who is depicted as a cold-blooded young politician in calculated contrast to his generous-souled elder brother; a contrast pointed, in comic terms, by Falstaff in his speech on the virtues of sack.

The campaign in Yorkshire is dramatically necessary to finish off the Percy plot which reaches its climax in Part I and to mark the clean-up of the internal situation before the accession of Henry V, who is to carry his victorious arms abroad. But it is not the chief theme of Part II, which is the triumph of Justice, that is of the principles of good government, in the breast of the heir to the throne, always remembering that to Elizabethans the person and mind of the Prince is the state. Yet this triumph is not in the main presented psychologically, as the result of an inward conflict, since Prince Hal, once again, is no Hamlet to debate his problems in the ears of the audience. Rather, Shakespeare adopts a device, strikingly similar to the machinery of the old morality: he brings embodiments of the two conflicting principles upon the stage, makes them engage in conversation together, so that we can judge between them for ourselves, and then shows us the Prince choosing between them. Thus during most of Part II the front of the stage is occupied by the portentous figures of Falstaff, who stands for Riot and Misrule, and of the Lord Chief Justice, the official representative of the Rule of Law. The legends tell us that the Prince once struck the Lord Chief Justice as he sat on his bench in court, and was committed to prison for so doing. There is nothing directly about this in Part I because, I think, Shakespeare wished to reserve Justice until Chivalry had been dealt with. Nor does he exhibit the incident in action, as the author of the old *Henry IV* play seems to have done.[20] But he makes Falstaff refer to it in express terms on the Lord Chief Justice's first entry in Part II; and he clearly assumed that his audience was perfectly familiar with the story. Once again, then, we do not *see* the Prince quarrelling with Justice; we are told at the beginning of Part II that he has quarrelled; and the fact, underlined and elaborated in the King's reproaches later, gives point and dramatic substance to the great reconciliation scene in the fifth act.

But the main reason, without a doubt, why Shakespeare keeps his Prince thus partially shrouded from our observation is in order to preserve our respect for his character. Just as in *Hamlet* the hero is never shown mad upon the stage but only reported as such to us through the mouths of other characters, so in *Henry IV* the 'truant to chivalry' is usually the perfect knight when before our eyes, while his quarrel with Justice is represented as an old unhappy far-off incident, a childish prank that the man has outgrown, though the opportunity of making full amends has not yet come. Indeed, after proving himself to himself on the field of Shrewsbury, the only thing that troubles his mind is the breach with the King, partly but not wholly healed by his conduct in battle. For the opinion of the world he shows not the slightest concern; but it is a real grief to him that he should be so much misconstrued in his wantonness by his father and sovereign.

Apart from his appearance in the Doll scene we only have two glimpses of him in Part II until he enters in the 'new and gorgeous garment, majesty' that is his by the King's death; and in both his thoughts are full of the sick father at Westminster. The first is the conversation he has with Poins on his return from Wales; a most revealing scene, since it exhibits him as now completely grown up, chafing at the worthlessness and uselessness of his companions, and with the ties of real affection that bind him to his dying father dragging at his heartstrings. As so often in Shakespeare, it is the death of a person dear to him, or the threat of it, that teaches a character to know himself.

All this is conveyed beneath a surface-play of light badinage between the two young men; the Prince shyly hinting to 'one it pleases me for fault of a better to call my friend' that he might weep for the King had not the 'vile company' he keeps deprived him of any reasonable pretext for showing his grief; and Poins, who completely misses the hint, rallying him as 'a most princely hypocrite' for affecting to mourn an event which promises the heir to the throne the consummation of his desires. 'It would be every man's thought', replies the Prince, with mingled bitterness and self-reproach, 'and thou art a blessed fellow to think as every man thinks. Never a man's thought in the world keeps the road-way better than thine. Every man would think me a hypocrite indeed.'[21] His youthful follies and heedless pursuit of pleasure have landed him in a false position, in what he is now acutely conscious is an intolerable position: he wakes up to find himself a traitor to all that he holds most dear in life, horribly 'engraffed' and allied with those who desire nothing better than the death of his own father! And how lonely the realization leaves him! He has no friends but these, while the father for whom his heart bleeds is estranged from him. Bardolph enters at this juncture with Falstaff's impudent letter, and the tone once again grows devil-may-care light with the project of catching the old rake in the act of cuddling his Doll; but what Hal now feels about the life that once seemed so amusing peeps out in his final speech, which comments upon Poins's suggestion that they shall disguise themselves as drawers. It falls in exceeding well with his mood of bitter cynicism to put off prince and assume pot-boy; 'for in everything the purpose must weigh with the folly'.[22]

Such are the thoughts, we must imagine, that accompany him until he confronts his father in the chamber of death at the end of the fourth act. But before that the attitude of the sick King himself towards his son is once again defined for us. We see him first at the beginning of act 3 crushed beneath the disease that afflicts his body and the no less grievous diseases that make foul the body of his kingdom; a prey to sleeplessness, that mocks the state of a royal bed-chamber, and yet wistfully hoping to accomplish after all the crusade which promises redemption for soul and kingdom alike. When he next appears, in act 4, scene 4, the rebels have been finally crushed in the north and Glendower is dead in Wales. The joyous tidings are too much for him, and he is borne swooning from the room. Before this, however, he has uttered significant speeches about his son and heir to the younger princes, Humphrey Duke of Gloucester and Thomas Duke of Clarence, who are in attendance. The chronicles tell us of jealousy and quarrels between Prince Hal and Prince Thomas. This is nothing to Shakespeare's purpose, but it no doubt suggested to his mind the speech in which the King advises Thomas how to handle his brother when he becomes king, a speech which I have also no doubt was written to give the audience an insight into the nature of this reserved hero that they could not otherwise have gained. The following lines are specially noteworthy in view of Hal's conduct immediately after his father's death:

> For he is gracious, if he be observed:
> He hath a tear for pity, and a hand
> Open as day for melting charity:
> Yet notwithstanding, being incensed, he's flint,
> As humorous as winter, and as sudden
> As flaws congealéd in the spring of day.[23]

The words refer, it should be noted, to the Prince's temperament only; in respect of his character the King continues to entertain the gloomiest possible notions. The young man's impulses might be generous, his qualities as a soldier most admirable, but his associates and moral disposition bode ill for the state. 'Therefore my grief', declares the King,

> Stretches itself beyond the hour of death.
>
> . . . .
>
> For when his headstrong riot hath no curb,
> When rage and hot blood are his counsellors,
> When means and lavish manners meet together,
> O, with what wings shall his affections fly
> Towards fronting peril and opposed decay ![24]

And so we come to the death-bed scene in which the last of many misunderstandings between Henry Bolingbroke and his greater son breaks forth like a tempest and is dispersed; a scene which, when fully apprehended, is surely one of the peaks of Shakespeare's dramatic achievement. The attendant circumstances are familiar to all: the crown upon the pillow of the sleeping King, the Prince entering to keep watch, his sudden assurance that the sleep has passed into death, his taking up the crown, his exit wearing it on his own head, the sick man's fierce anger upon awakening, and finally the explanation and reconciliation. I content myself with a few points by way of emphasis and comment. First, then, it is important to grasp what the crown means to the heir who tries it on. He calls it a troublesome bedfellow, a 'polished perturbation, golden care',[25] which has worn his father out. In other words, it is the weight of it that fills his thought, not its splendour or the opportunities it affords for power or self-indulgence. And that is why he puts it on, not in pride, still less in eager grasping, but to feel this weight pressing upon his brow; as he himself explains,

> To try with it, as with an enemy
> That had before my face murdered my father,
> The quarrel of a true inheritor.[26]

The burden of kingship, which is the theme of his meditations throughout the play of *Henry V*, is what the 'golden rigol' means to him even before it comes to be his. In the second place, the assertion of his rights and duties, which follows, is intended as a solemn act of dedication. As he sets the crown upon his head, he proclaims with religious fervour:

> Lo, where it sits,
> Which God shall guard! and put the world's whole strength
> Into one giant arm, it shall not force
> This lineal honour from me: this from thee
> Will I to mine leave, as 'tis left to me.[27]

After which he falls to his knees by the dead man, as he supposes him to be, and remains a moment in prayer before walking out of the room, shaken with sobs and as in a dream; the crown, now forgotten, still upon his head. For—and this is my third point— the profound grief of the Prince, evident in the text both from his own protestations later and from the report of Warwick who finds him in the next room,

> Washing with kindly [i.e. filial] tears his gentle cheeks,

should be made clear *in action* by the bedside upon the stage. Otherwise one of the greatest moments of the play will be ruined and the Prince's state of mind but half understood.

That the audience should be left in no doubt about it is the more necessary because the King on awakening places the worst possible construction upon the disappearance of the crown, the crown to secure which he had risked so much in this life and the next, and for which he imagines the thirst of others to equal that of his own. Once more he charges his heir with thoughts of treachery, with desiring to hasten his death, with posting in indecent haste to steal

> that which after some few hours
> Were thine without offence.[28]

The guilty conscience of a usurper, the distempered fancies of an invalid, and the genuine solicitude of a true governor of his people combine to give out these fumes of suspicion, and the bitter speech culminates in a picture of the future of England almost as terrible as that which Ulysses draws in *Troilus and Cressida* of a world in which 'Degree' has been overthrown.

> Harry the Fifth is crowned! up, vanity!
> Down royal state! all you sage counsellors, hence!
> And to the English court assemble now
> From every region, apes of idleness!
> Now, neighbour confines, purge you of your scum:
> Have you a ruffian that will swear, drink, dance,
> Revel the night, rob, murder and commit
> The oldest sins the newest kind of ways?
> Be happy, he will trouble you no more:
> England shall double gild his treble guilt,
> England shall give him office, honour, might:
> For the fifth Harry from curbed licence plucks
> The muzzle of restraint, and the wild dog
> Shall flesh his tooth on every innocent.
> O, my poor kingdom! sick with civil blows
> When that my care could not withhold thy riots,
> What wilt thou do when Riot is thy care?
> O, thou wilt be a wilderness again,
> Peopled with wolves, thy old inhabitants![29]

Shakespeare penned these words with a double purpose: first to give Hal an occasion for his loyal and large-hearted reply, completely satisfying to his father and still further exalting him in our estimation; and secondly to show us what would have followed had the Prince chosen Vanity instead of Government, Falstaff and not the Lord Chief Justice. The glimpse, it will be noticed, is a glimpse of Hell, of Hell not so much for the Prodigal Prince as for the unhappy country over which he was called to rule, since what is at stake in this morality play is the salvation of England itself.

At this stage, I submit, having followed the action of the play, so far as it concerns the Prince, up to the end of act 4, we are not only prepared for him to reject Falstaff when the moment comes, but willing to accept the rejection as both just and inevitable. We have not, however, heard the fat man's side of the story, because in concentrating our attention upon Hal's doings and character we have had to pass over most of the Falstaff scenes after the middle of Part I. Before we go on, then, to consider the fifth act of Part II, which culminates in the rejection and all which that implies, we must return to the fortunes of Falstaff, retracing our steps to the moment at which we left him in Part I when, entrusted by Hal with a charge of foot, he takes service for the wars as a captain whose first duty is to raise his own company. And as we follow him to Shrewsbury and back to London, to Justice Shallow's and Gaultree Forest, and once again to Gloucestershire on his way to Westminster, let us ever bear in mind the charge which modern criticism has laid at Shakespeare's door, namely that he has caused us to fall so deeply in love with the rogue that we find his rejection intolerable, however much it may be justified upon grounds of conscience and of state.

CHAPTER V

FALSTAFF HIGH ON FORTUNE'S WHEEL

At the end of chapter III we left Falstaff waiting for his breakfast
at the Boar's Head, and feeling a trifle cheap, or as he puts it
'withered', on the morning after the night before. Sir John Bracy's
news of the insurrection, together perhaps with a touch of cramp
from sleeping on the boards behind the arras, has made him an
early stirrer, and he is now in battle-dress, with a captain's
truncheon at his girdle. Presently Hal and Poins enter, marching
single file; Falstaff and Bardolph fall in beside them, Falstaff
'playing upon his truncheon like a fife'; and after a digression on
the loss of his grandfather's seal-ring, the Prince tells him he is to
have a charge of foot, bids him meet him next day for money and
instructions, and then hurries away upon urgent business of state.
From this moment Falstaff's fortunes are bound up with military
service, and if we are to get an idea of his quality as a soldier the
two campaigns in which he is successively engaged may conveniently be considered together. Before, however, we follow
our 'tall gentleman and most gallant leader' to the wars, it will be
well to take a look at literary and dramatic antecedents which may
have influenced at once Shakespeare's delineation of him in this
role and the expectations of the audience.

The Classical Braggart and the Old Soldier

Although Queen Elizabeth generally managed to avoid open war
with her enemies, there was plenty of fighting during her reign
in Ireland and, of an unofficial character, on the continent; and the
London which first saw Falstaff on the stage was full of soldiers,
old and young. By creating the fat knight, therefore, and making
him captain in the infantry, Shakespeare did for his generation—

though in an incomparably more artistic fashion—very much what Bruce Bairnsfather did with his 'Old Bill' for those of us who lived through the War of 1914–18. Such comic soldiers have probably been thrown up by every great war in which we have been engaged, since they appeal to a permanent whimsy in the national character: while the Germans glorify war, we have always preferred to joke about it. In renaissance drama, however, as was noted in chapter II, the comic soldier was expected to conform to the traditional type of crude braggart who struts through Roman comedy, and had nothing characteristically English about him. Three at least of these are found in pre-Shakespearian English plays, Ralph Roister Doister, Captain Crackstone in Munday's *Two Italian Gentlemen*, and Basilisco in Kyd's *Soliman and Perseda*, while Shakespeare has his versions in Pistol, belonging to the play before us, and the Parolles of *All's Well that Ends Well*. Then there is the brilliantly conceived Bobadill in Jonson's *Every Man in his Humour*, Bessus in Beaumont and Fletcher's *A King and no King*, and so on. Falstaff too belongs to the category in the opinion of many; indeed, some regard the *miles gloriosus* as the clue to his whole character.[1] Yet one has only to compare him with the examples just mentioned to see at once that, while there are traces of the braggart in his behaviour, he is a different kind of soldier altogether. This difference may be put in a sentence: whereas the others, from the original in Plautus downwards, are all *sham* soldiers, who brag of their exploits beforehand and are exposed to open and apparent shame when their pretensions are put to trial by battle, Falstaff is, as Morgann first called him, 'the *old* soldier',[2] up to all the tricks of the trade, which he has presumably learnt from previous campaigns, and very well knows how to turn to his own advantage. The touchstone here, as in other dramatic problems, is the attitude of the audience. To what emotions did Shakespeare appeal in the incident of Parolles and the drum, or Ben Jonson in that of the beating of Bobadill? Scorn and derision, without a doubt. Falstaff, on the other hand, is subject to no such exposure, even in the Boar's Head scene after Gad's Hill; and our response to his antics on the battlefield, for the realities of which he displays a healthy respect that no soldier will fail to appreciate, is one of delighted amusement at his circumspection and resource.

What we may call Falstaff's normal attitude towards war is revealed in the welcome he gives to Hal's announcement that he has procured him a charge of foot:

> I would it had been of horse. Where shall I find one that can steal well? O, for a fine thief, of the age of two and twenty or thereabouts! I am heinously unprovided. Well, God be thanked for these rebels, they offend none but the virtuous; I laud them, I praise them.[3]

In other words, 'I see this is the time that the unjust man doth thrive;[4] and if only I had a horse and a nimble-fingered batman, I might thrive well enough'. War is his great opportunity, a heaven-sent palliative—cure was beyond even Heaven's power— for that consumption of the purse which ever afflicts him. He is the Old Soldier on the make, or in a state of perpetual repair, and Shakespeare exhibits him busy upon a number of disreputable devices for raising money, which were attributed, in whispers, or even at times in printed books, to old soldiers in Elizabeth's reign, most of them connected with the recruitment of troops. For, there being neither standing army nor professional soldiery, an officer of those days, that is a gentleman bearing Her Majesty's commission, had to impress his company before he could command it.

Falstaff, says Hal, will be told next day in Temple Hall how many men he is to enlist and given 'money and order for their furniture', that is to say for their uniforms and equipment. And, as we find Bardolph later acting as quartermaster and issuing 'coats' to the recruits in Gloucestershire,[5] we are at liberty to suspect that the purchase of such 'furniture' was a source of profit, some of which stuck to his greasy palm. But the favourite way for a captain to make money, one notorious enough to receive special mention in an act of Parliament passed in 1557, was to enrol well-to-do men, known to be reluctant to serve, and then allow them

to buy themselves out at the highest price they could be induced
to pay.[6] In the Coventry scene Falstaff confides to the audience
that he had first enlisted 150 'warm slaves' of this type, making
over £300 on the lot; after which he had filled up his muster-roll
by impressing another 150, whom he now commands, this time
the sweepings of the highways and the prisons. 'I did never see
such pitiful rascals' protests the Prince, as they march into view;
to which Falstaff retorts, 'Tut, tut, good enough to toss, food for
powder, food for powder—they'll fill a pit as well as better'. It
is a famous piece of cynicism; but seriously intended. For he leads
them into the hottest part of the battle at Shrewsbury, where all
but three are killed, with the object, well understood by spectators
of the time, of pocketing the pay of the dead.[7] Commenting
on this incident, Morgann and Bradley account it unto him for
prowess that he *led* his men where they were peppered, and did
not send them.[8] But Elizabethans well knew that it was a common,
if not the usual, practice for an officer of the army 'to offer his
men to the face of the enemy' and then 'take his leave (under pretence to fetch supplies)'.[9] In the campaign of Part II he is commissioned 'to take up soldiers in counties'[10] as he travels north, and
so we get in the first scene at Justice Shallow's even more damnable
misuse of the king's press, with the addition of fresh dodges. To
Falstaff war is as welcome as harvest to the husbandman.

He went to battle for what he could get out of it, and preferred
to be paid in gold not lead, if the latter could be avoided. Risks
must be run, of course; but life was full of risks, on the highway
as on the battlefield; and there were ways of fighting shy without
incurring the charge of cowardice, which might have ruined the
good will, so to speak, of a lucrative business. One of these, a
simple trick, was to arrive on the scene of action at the latest
convenient moment.

> To the latter end of a fray and the beginning of a feast
> Fits a dull fighter and a keen guest

is his jingling comment on Prince Hal's instructions to hasten, when he finds him loitering on the road to Shrewsbury.[11] And though, as we shall see, it does not suit Shakespeare's book to have him miss any of that battle, he does not turn up at Gaultree Forest until the pursuit of the rebels is as good as finished. Whereupon Prince John, who knows the kind of fellow he is talking to, raps him over the knuckles with

> Now, Falstaff, where have *you* been all this while?
> When everything is ended, then you come:
> These tardy tricks of yours will, on my life,
> One time or other break some gallows' back.[12]

The rascal is able triumphantly to counter this by producing the distinguished prisoner, Sir John Colevile of the Dale. Nor is the capture just a piece of comic extravaganza; a late arrival might reckon on picking up a fugitive or two; and there may well have been precedents in Tudor engagements for Falstaff's luck.

When, on the other hand, an action cannot be avoided, as at Shrewsbury, then 'the better part of valour is discretion'.[13] Some quarters of the field would be less unhealthy than others; and the really dangerous people in the enemy's forces might be given a wide berth. When the Prince begs him for the loan of his sword, he refuses—unwilling to be left thus defenceless—on the jesting plea that he needs it for the 'piercing' of Percy; but he adds in an aside,

> If he *do* come in my way, so. If he do not, if *I* come in his willingly, let him make a carbonado of me. I like not such grinning honour as Sir Walter hath. Give me life, which if I can save, so; if not, honour comes unlooked for.[14]

'Surely the man...who meditates thus', protests Bradley, 'is not what we commonly call a coward.'[15] No, but as surely such a man will not fight longer than he sees reason. And when fighting seems demanded, he will put a bold face upon it, strike a blow or two, and leave the rest to chance, cunning, or—if there be nothing else for it—flight. In the engagement on Gad's Hill, flight could not be helped, since the others had fled already, and the odds—two buckram men upon poor old Jack—overwhelming. In the passage at arms with Douglas, flight at the mere sight of whom might have been almost excusable, he nevertheless puts up a show of resolution, though he falls down and shams dead immediately after. In the third and last encounter, that with Colevile, the enemy like a kind fellow gives himself away gratis, so that we have nothing more than the first phase, the brazen front and the would-be intimidating words. But had Colevile not surrendered at once, we may surmise that another sham death would have followed the exchange of a few blows. Such is the pattern of his skill as a fighting man: valour first, discretion after.

The kind of soldier who *likes* fighting, who actually seeks out champions to strive with, puzzles him. 'But, tell me Hal,' he asks, peering into the Prince's face, 'art thou not horribly afeard? thou, being heir-apparent, could the world pick thee out three such enemies again, as that fiend Douglas, that spirit Percy, and that devil Glendower? doth not thy blood thrill at it?' 'Not a whit, i'faith,' is the reply, 'I lack some of thy instinct.'[16] Yet the question is prompted by curiosity, not cowardice. What Hal calls honour is as unintelligible to him, as virtue is to Iago, while the honour Hotspur speaks of is just moonshine. The famous catechism, as we have seen, expresses the Falstaffian creed.[17]

Falstaff, then, is no *miles gloriosus*, though he is ready to play the part, after Gad's Hill and again at Shrewsbury, for the Prince's amusement. Rather, he is Shakespeare's improvement upon that ancient stock figure, a transformation of the sawdust theatrical puppet into a creature for ever palpitating with flesh and blood; mountains of flesh, geysers of blood! More than this, the incarnation is mere English. Our drama had taken over the military braggadocio from Roman and Italian comedy, as it took over other types, such as the pedant, the charlatan, or the garrulous old woman, almost automatically or at least in deferential imitation; Shakespeare found it lying in his path, moulded it to his own use, and made something fresh, living, native out of it. The old *miles* had been popular enough on the London stage, and remained popular; it was Shakespeare who first gave fighting men in the audience a character they could recognize, one they often met in the field and at the tavern; the Old Soldier, raised to the highest power of comedy.

THE 'DAY'S SERVICE' AT SHREWSBURY, AND ITS 'REWARD'

But 'old soldier' is not the same as 'good soldier'; and the attempt of Morgann and others to make out Falstaff to be a warrior who had for years enjoyed a considerable military reputation rests upon a number of mistaken notions, some about what Shakespeare tells us, and some about the very nature of drama. That he should be present, for instance, at the council of war in the royal tent before the battle of Shrewsbury, is due, not to his standing with the higher command, but simply to the fact that Shakespeare needed him on the stage at that point, chiefly for the sake of the comic prologue to the battle, his speech on Honour, with which the scene closes.[18] Similarly Bradley's statement that 'when he saw Henry and Hotspur fighting, Falstaff, instead of making off in a panic, stayed to take his chance if Hotspur should be the victor',[19] ignores not only his express declaration of contrary intentions, quoted two pages back, but the fact that if he is to encounter 'that devil Douglas' and establish his false claim to the slaying of Hotspur, he must be brought into the thick of the fight and be shown present at the combat between Percy and the Prince. There is indeed nothing whatever in Part I to indicate that Falstaff possesses a military reputation of any kind. Certainly, Hal and Poins do not credit him with one; and if the former procures him his charge of foot, that is the least he could do to get him to Shrewsbury, where Shakespeare required his presence.[20] It is from Part II that Morgann draws his evidence, such as it is. And the 'why' for this is plain as way to parish church, though, owing to the habit of knowing and judging by what is *going* to happen,[21] all the critics seem to have missed it. Falstaff only becomes what Bradley calls 'a person of consideration in the army' after the battle of Shrewsbury, after, that is, he has slain, or helped to slay, the mighty Hotspur, chief of the rebels. In Part I he is Jack Falstaff with his familiars; in Part II he is Sir John with all Europe.

The words of the messenger, who gives old Northumberland tidings of the death of his son, show us that the true facts of the fight with Harry Monmouth had been observed by at least one man. But no other witness is quoted and, as we have seen, not even King Henry himself appears to realize what has taken place.[22] The Prince is as good as his word; he gilds Falstaff's lie with the happiest terms at his command; and the Lord Chief Justice's grudging admission: 'Your day's service at Shrewsbury hath a little gilded over your night's exploits on Gad's Hill'[23] assures us that the gilding had passed current for true gold. Shakespeare leaves the particulars vague—the more a dramatist defines the less freedom he allows to himself—but makes it certain that, whether wholly or in part, the glory of Hotspur's overthrow belongs, not to Harry Monmouth, but to his 'brawn, the hulk Sir John'.[24]

Thus the 'established fame and reputation of military merit'[25] claimed for Falstaff rests solely upon his 'day's service at Shrewsbury', which explains all the 'facts' alleged in support of it. The special mention of his capture in the false report of the battle that first reaches the ears of Northumberland,[26] the dozen captains,

> Bare-headed, sweating, knocking at the taverns,
> And asking every one for Sir John Falstaff,[27]

who was dallying with Doll when he should have been well on the way to York; the summons to court;[28] the deference with which Justice Shallow receives him and his man Bardolph;[29] the readiness of that doughty rebel Sir John Colevile to yield himself at the mere sight of his belly;[30] all are accounted for by the 'indecent'[31] stab which the dastard gives the corpse of Hotspur as it lies bleeding on the stricken field. In a word, his military reputation is not only complete bogus, but one of the best jokes in the whole drama. By a combination of luck, brutality, and impudence the Old Soldier crops the flower of English chivalry and flaunts it in his bonnet.

The critics, blind to all this, have with one exception[32] been equally blind to what follows. For observe that the imposture, once accepted by the world, works like yeast in the mind of the impostor himself, much as Maria's letter works upon that of Malvolio; and so explains the difference which many have noticed, in a puzzled fashion, between the Falstaffs of the two Parts. Consider first the situation in which the battle of Shrewsbury leaves the round knave. His claim to the honours of the field, though jestingly phrased, is seriously advanced, and an ample reward demanded. 'There is Percy!' he cries, pitching the body off his back at the feet of the amazed Prince, who having just breathed an epitaph over the prostrate form of his 'old acquaintance', thinks for a moment that a ghost stands before him; 'There is Percy! If your father will do me any honour, so; if not, let him kill the next Percy himself. I look to be either earl or duke, I can assure you.'[33] And having secured a promise of support from the good-humoured Prince, who then goes off with his brother John to survey the battlefield, Falstaff concludes the scene with this brief soliloquy, which forms his last words in Part I:

I'll follow, as they say, for reward. He that rewards me, God reward him! If I do grow great, I'll grow less, for I'll purge, and leave sack, and live cleanly as a nobleman should do.[34]

As far as I am aware, no one has ever asked what reward, if any, he receives, or whether he ever attempts to make good this hint of adjusting his behaviour to his increased importance in the public eye. Yet Shakespeare develops both points in the very next Falstaff scene. Why have they been overlooked? Because that scene, being the second scene of Part II, has been thought of as *belonging to another play*, only distantly connected with words and events at Shrewsbury, of which we read in the penultimate scene of Part I. On the other hand, once the connection is made, it becomes obvious that Falstaff's conduct at the beginning of Part II will be inexplicable to an audience, unless they have his exact situation and actual words at Shrewsbury fresh in mind. In short, Part II was written to be played immediately, or at not more than twenty-four hours' interval, after Part I. It is the most telling proof among many of the theatrical and dramatic unity of the two parts.

And when we turn to consider this second scene of Part II, we are met with a transformed Falstaff, a transformation which should, I believe, be marked in the way such things are apt to be marked in the theatre, by a startling change of costume. 'Enter Sir John alone, with his page bearing his sword and buckler' is the stage-direction the Quarto gives for him. The diminutive page, probably played by the same boy who takes the part of tiny sprightly Maria in *Twelfth Night*, has, we shortly afterwards learn, been presented by the Prince to serve as squire to Falstaff's new-furbished knighthood; with an eye, as Falstaff himself points out, to the ludicrous contrast the pair will make, as the boy waits at his heels. The effect is all the more ludicrous that the little squire comes on carrying the immense sword and buckler which denote his master's knightly dignity. Falstaff does not carry his own sword for an excellent reason. He cannot, because he enters hobbling upon a stick; he is, in fact, playing the wounded hero, though we discover at the end of the scene that the true cause of his halting is gout, or pox, and that he is turning 'diseases to commodity'. And not being able to carry a sword, he is dressed, no longer as a soldier, but as Elizabethan gentlemen dressed in civil life. In short, I suggest, his first appearance on the stage since Shrewsbury shows him to us as the complete courtier, or as we should now put it, man about town; that is to say, fashionably, fantastically, hilariously decked out, according to the very latest and most foppish cut, yards and yards and yards of it, with some absurdity of a cap to crown the sartorial edifice. All his entries were, no doubt, the subject of much thought on the part of the presiding genius of the tiring-room, and such a costume would bring the house down before he opened his lips. It would carry important dramatic implications also, since it immediately apprises the audience, reminded of Shrewsbury by the wounded hero touch, of the changed status and social aspirations foreshadowed at the end of Part I, while it provides a visible focus for the hints of this change to be now dropped.

For, whatever be his costume, the dialogue shows without a doubt that he is cutting a figure in the world. The resolution to 'purge', made on the battlefield, has developed: he has taken to consulting doctors and even to reading Galen on his own account.[35] And to be a valetudinarian is to display the hall-mark of gentility, as we have already learnt from Hotspur's popinjay,[36] if we need to be taught so persistent a fact of human nature. He has, also, a fashionable complaint, whichever of the two it may be he suffers from; and the evident irritability of his temper, with a visible twinge or two perhaps, should inform the audience, long before he names the alternative possibilities, that the bandages about the foot conceal an inflammation not caused by wounds. In a word, there is something of the gouty colonel of a later age in this old soldier and Shrewsbury champion. The Prince, he testily remarks, is almost out of his favour, which implies maybe that the 'reward' hoped for in Part I has not come up to expectations. We are told towards the end of the scene that it is a 'pension', and its inadequacy is revealed by the state of the pensioner's purse. Yet a pension, even if always spent before receipt, has its uses, at any rate as a basis for credit; and it is clear that he is busy equipping himself on the strength of it. The outburst against that 'whoreson Achitophel' Master Dommelton, who refuses to accept Bardolph as a surety in the matter of a purchase of satin for a short cloak and slops—the first really ill-tempered speech we have had from the jovial knight—is an indication that he is furnishing himself with a wardrobe; and Mistress Quickly gives further hints of the same sort in his next scene when she speaks of his dining with Master Smooth, the silkman, and of his calling on the way thither at Pye Corner to buy a saddle, no doubt for the horse he has previously commissioned Bardolph to purchase in Smithfield. He even seems to be contemplating marriage, though apparently hesitating whether to bestow the style of 'Lady Falstaff' on Mistress Quickly, old Mistress Ursula, whom he had weekly sworn to marry since he perceived the first white hair on his chin, or some proper gentle-woman from the stews. Here is a Falstaff moving in a very different element from that of highway robbery and purse-taking, to which he belongs in Part I.

'IF I DO GROW GREAT, I'LL GROW LESS'

He is different in other ways too. There is nothing in Part II to equal the sheer delight of the first Boar's-Head scene. Yet he is no less brilliant or entertaining on the whole. But the entertainment has shifted its centre of gravity. We laugh as much as ever, but no longer in the heart, or with the thought 'were't not for laughing, I should pity him'. We find his wit no less fascinating, but he begins to inspire less affection. His impudence and effrontery increase: he remains as ever imperturbable, and the 'gout' after doing duty in the first scene is heard of no more; but with our pleasure at his sallies and our admiration for his intellect there is mingled a spice, and presently more than a spice, of critical detach-ment. The difference, which is subtle but profound, felt only gradually but becoming more and more unmistakable, is best described by saying that he passes from the realm of the humorous into that of the comic.

Falstaff is his own chief theme throughout, and the change just noted is well exemplified by comparing his treatment of this theme in the two Parts. In Part I the staple of his jesting is his moral weaknesses and physical disabilities. He is ready with mock-apology for his sins and for his size, with affectations of holiness and patter about repentance. It is sighing and grief that has blown him up like a bladder; he has more flesh than another man and therefore more frailty; and if he has forgotten what the inside of a church is made of, it is company, villainous company, that has been the spoil of him. The appeal to our laughter is made in the name of helplessness, bodily and spiritual. We are asked to con-template him staggering along life's way, with his broken wind,

although eight yards of its uneven ground is to him what a pil-
grimage of threescore and ten miles would be to anyone else; and
which villain among us is stony-hearted enough to turn a deaf ear,
sheer blarney as we know it all to be? And there is a subtler side
to it, well brought out by John Bailey. 'What specially wins our
love' for Falstaff, he declares, is that he, 'at his most triumphant
times, is triumphant at his own expense. If he did not know that
he was a gross tun of flesh, a drunkard, a coward, and a liar, we
should know it much more and love him much less. Here, as
in religion, the way of confession is the way of forgiveness. And
forgiving is very near loving.' [37]

Both apology and confession belong to Part I; not a trace of
either is to be found in Part II; even the plea of old age, which he
turns to such eloquent account in the address 'in the behalf of that
Falstaff' at the Boar's Head, is disclaimed, except once in a tender
moment with Doll. When Bradley writes, 'Instead of being comic
to you and serious to himself, he is more ludicrous to himself than
to you; and he makes himself out more ludicrous than he is in
order that he and others may laugh',[38] he is speaking, as he usually
is, of the Falstaff of Part I. Of him the words are true enough; but
the Falstaff of Part II *is* more ludicrous to us than to himself, while
the only sport he makes of his own person is the picture he evokes
of himself walking before his page 'like a sow that hath overwhelmed all her litter but one', and a couple of quibbling asides
about his waist and his 'gravy' in the first scene with the Lord
Chief Justice. Instead of exploiting or lamenting his weakness,
he proclaims his wit. The new note—may we not call it the note
of comic hubris?—is heard in his first words:

Men of all sorts take a pride to gird at me: the brain of this foolish-
compounded clay, man, is not able to invent anything that intends to
laughter, more than I invent, or is invented on me: I am not only witty
in myself, but the cause that wit is in other men.[39]

How often is that quoted in the *laudes Falstaffii* which too many
know better than Shakespeare's *Henry IV*! And no wonder, for

we have only to change the first into the third person and it might have been written in Falstaff's honour by Morgann or Bradley. Yet self-praise, apart from tributes to his own valour, not intended seriously, is something we have not had from Falstaff before. And I feel sure that Shakespeare gives him this piece of complacency by way of throwing, as Meredith would say, the oblique light of the comic muse upon him. If not, why does the fat man continue in the same vein, with scornful and patronizing remarks about the Prince, the victor of Shrewsbury, who out of pure friendship and kindness of heart has resigned all claim to the overthrow of Hotspur and has countenanced the fraud which is the only basis of those present pretensions?

As to the pretensions themselves, listen to the old turkey-cock strutting and puffing before the Lord Chief Justice, who makes polite reference to his impending service under Prince John:

> There is not a dangerous action can peep out his head but I am thrust upon it. Well, I cannot last for ever, but it was alway yet the trick of our English nation, if they have a good thing, to make it too common. If ye will needs say I am an old man, you should give me rest: I would to God my name were not so terrible to the enemy as it is.[40]

Only half of this, of course, is believed by the speaker; but that half is enough to set the comic muse smiling. The words might almost have been written by Bernard Shaw for one of his numskull Englishmen.

Falstaff, Bradley tells us again, is able to reduce 'the would-be serious things of life' to nothing by means of his wit and his gaiety, and so 'to walk about free and rejoicing'. True enough in the first Boar's Head scene; but in the scenes of Part II he is no longer free, for the simple reason that now he has begun to take something seriously, namely his own career and ambitions. It is all intensely funny, of course, and the wit, I repeat, is as brilliant as ever. But the best joke of all, a joke altogether lost if Part II be not enjoyed as an immediate continuation of Part I, is that the old mock-maudlin highwayman should have blossomed out into this preposterous, self-satisfied, pink of gentility. And the joke is one which Falstaff, for the first time in the play, is himself unconscious of.

Yet we too remain unconscious of where Shakespeare is taking us, until well on in Part II. In Part I Falstaff is the great Boon Companion of modern literature; by the end of its sequel he is seen to be an impossible companion for a king of England. But he remains the same exceedingly entertaining person throughout, with a like genius at command; and though (prying into the secrets of Shakespeare's art, in order to clear it of misunderstanding) I have put my finger on the false claim to Hotspur's corpse as the point at which the change of emphasis begins, no watcher in the theatre, or reader following the play scene by scene for the mere enjoyment of it, will detect this, or even become aware except insensibly that a change in his attitude is taking place at all, so delicately and by such fine degrees are the readjustments made upon the scales. Let him pass straight from the tavern scene after Gad's Hill to the finale outside Westminster Abbey, which is virtually what Bradley and his followers do, and he will, like them, find the rejection an outrage; whereas the same rejection, taken at its right point of dramatic time, that is after the whole play has been experienced in the order and under the conditions Shakespeare intended, becomes unexceptionable, even a happy solution.

Bradley sees clearly what Shakespeare had to do. He even admits that in Part II it was his purpose 'to work a gradual change in our feelings towards Falstaff, and to tinge the humorous atmosphere more and more deeply with seriousness',[41] and he notes many of the later stages in the attempt to carry this purpose out. The attempt fails, however, in his opinion, because the dramatist found himself incapable of alienating our sympathies from a character, in the creation of which he had 'overreached himself'.[42] 'If', he declares,

as the Second Part of *Henry IV* advanced, he had clouded over Falstaff's humour so heavily that the man of genius turned into the Falstaff of *The Merry Wives*, we should have witnessed his rejection without a pang.

This Shakespeare was too much of an artist to do—though even in this way he did something—and without this device he could not succeed.[43]

That the 'gradual change in our feelings' is aesthetic as well as moral, comic before it becomes serious, altogether escapes him, since he fails to catch sight of the nimbus of ridicule that shines ever more brightly about the fat man's bald crown as Part II proceeds. It was not necessary to transform Falstaff into the fatuous laughing-stock of *The Merry Wives* in order to make a success of *Henry IV*. Shakespeare is a greater artist than Bradley takes him for, and knows subtler ways of regulating the sympathies of his audience. At the beginning of *Richard II* he presents us with the portrait of an insolent young tyrant; before the play is over he has us mourning the same man as St Richard, King and Martyr. With Falstaff the process is reversed: our sympathies, at their height in Part I, have largely ebbed away by the end of Part II. But, though a narrow examination can fix the turning-point at the passage from one to the other, it is, like the turn of the tides, invisible to the eye of a spectator.

In the theatre, which is the ultimate tribunal for matters of this kind, the question is how Falstaff should be acted, even what are to be the tones of his voice. Bradley implies that he should be played in Part II exactly as he was in Part I, since he draws the evidence upon which he builds up his conception of the character indiscriminately from both parts, without noticing traits which mark a change. Thus he refuses to see—or rather, to hear—his pettiness, his irascibility, his self-importance, and what Hudson well calls 'the arrogance' of his 'utter impunity'.[44] And his followers are equally blind or deaf to such tones.[45] The issue must, I say, be left to the players in the last resort. But an encouraging feature of twentieth-century Shakespearian productions is that the players have begun to look for help to the scholars, while the scholars, on their side, are increasingly inclined to learn from the players. The present account of how one scholar believes Falstaff should be

played in Part II is offered as a modest contribution to this sym-
posium.

Before I continue, however, there are still one or two remarks
of a sign-post character to be made. In the first place, as most
critics have observed, whereas in Part I Falstaff is usually shown
in the Prince's company, in Part II Shakespeare keeps their paths
so far apart that they only meet once, before the final encounter
outside the Abbey. This separation, dramatically accounted for as
due to action by the King, taken at the suggestion of the Lord Chief
Justice,[46] is technically required for the presentation, not only, as
we have seen, of the Prince's character, but also of Falstaff's. It is
often remarked that the Prince's wit is at its best when Falstaff is
there to bring it out; it is equally true that the presence of the
Prince is the stimulus which transports Falstaff, and us with him,
into that sphere where he moves as the happiest of jesters. He is,
in short, at his most enchanting, when he is enchanting his patron.
In Part II his intellectual powers are no less, but are devoted to
other ends. In the second place, then, while we see a good deal
more of him in Part II than in Part I, what we see may be called
the normal Falstaff, the Falstaff who has to live by the clock, the
Falstaff of mean shifts, who abuses the King's press more damnably
than ever, who has all the tricks of the sharper or 'cheater' at his
fingers' ends. Thirdly, the touch of hubris already noted grows
more marked as scene follows scene, until we become acutely
conscious that the old scoundrel is riding for a fall. And, lastly, to
underline all this, we find him brought into contact with the only
man in England he really fears, the Lord Chief Justice.

THE LORD CHIEF JUSTICE AND MISTRESS
DOROTHY TEARSHEET

The role of the Lord Chief Justice cannot, I think, be given its full
dramatic weight by anyone who has not seen Part II in the theatre.
Certainly, I had no notion of its importance until I witnessed a
performance in April 1939 at the Schiller Theater, Berlin, with

Heinrich George playing Falstaff, and playing him superbly. As far as my knowledge goes, the only writer hitherto to realize the significance of the Justice is Miss Muriel Bradbrook, who makes the interesting suggestion that 'for the purposes of the stage' he 'walked around in Cheapside in full robes of office' when the play was originally produced.[47] Apart from his symbolical function in this Tudor morality, here for the first time in the drama is a personage whom Falstaff hates and detests. It takes him all he knows to keep his temper when they meet, and the urbane old gentleman crosses his path at awkward moments. The effect on the stage of this figure of majestic dignity and self-composure, and of Falstaff's unconcealed antagonism, is most striking. With those calm eyes upon him his 'fool-born jests' seem to break and fall away, like spume beneath a rock; and we recognize that there is, after all, Law in England, and that Riot, for all his gaiety and impudence, has met his match. Speaking of the 'comic world', with its 'humorous atmosphere', in which he asserts Falstaff moves in both parts, Bradley writes: 'The intervention of a serious spirit breaks up such a world, and would destroy our pleasure in Falstaff's company. Accordingly, through the greater part of these dramas Shakespeare carefully confines this spirit to the scenes of war and policy, and dismisses it entirely in the humorous parts.'[48] Had he ever seen the play upon the stage, he must, I think, have observed that, on the contrary, Shakespeare embodies this 'serious spirit' in the person of the Lord Chief Justice, and that the character is made to intervene, solely in order to disturb, if not exactly to destroy, our pleasure in Falstaff's company. We begin to feel this at their first encounter.

Shakespeare often expresses in the words and actions of one character what he intends to make us feel, without intellectual formulation, about another. And by throwing Falstaff, at the opening of Part II, into the company of the Lord Chief Justice he brings him under the eyes of someone who sees him exactly as he is and will not hesitate to put it into words. The wicked old rascal does his best to avoid a meeting. Forgetting his gout, he bolts down a side-alley directly he catches sight of his enemy; he feigns deafness to his serving-man's calls, and when the 'young knave' plucks him by the sleeve, pretends to take him for a beggar; lastly, finding he can no longer refuse to see the great man himself, he still keeps him at arm's length with talk of his lordship's health, of the King's return from Wales, of the royal apoplexy, of the nature of that disease, and so forth. Nor should the venom in his apparently innocent enquiries be overlooked: were the apoplexy he harps upon to prove fatal, the office, if not the life, of the judge might lie at the mercy of the heir apparent's favourite. For dexterous evasion and brilliant effrontery, Falstaff is at the very top of his form. Yet neither evasion nor effrontery will serve; in the end he is compelled to stand and listen.

My lord is courteous, for he is a great gentleman; on the whole, even lenient, since good soldiers are precious in times of danger, and this one is reputed to have done signal service at Shrewsbury; so that, in reply to the thrasonical brag already quoted, he dismisses him with the mild charge, 'Well, be honest, and God bless your expedition'. But he looks his man straight in the eyes, and is firm throughout, meeting the rogue's insolence with a sharp reminder that, while he holds his office, he has pains and penalties at his disposal. 'This apoplexy', Falstaff insists, 'as I take it, is a kind of lethargy, an't please your lordship', well knowing that nothing pleases his lordship less, 'a kind of sleeping in blood, a whoreson tingling'. Upon which follows this dialogue:

Lord Chief Justice. What tell you me of it? be it as it is.

Falstaff. It hath it original from much grief, from study and perturbation of the brain. I have read the cause of his effects in Galen, it is a kind of deafness.

Lord Chief Justice. I think you are fallen into the disease, for you hear not what I say to you.

Falstaff. Very well, my lord, very well—rather, an't please you, it is the disease of not listening, the malady of not marking, that I am troubled withal.

Lord Chief Justice. To punish you by the heels would amend the attention of your ears, and I care not if I do become your physician.

Falstaff. I am as poor as Job, my lord, but not so patient. Your lordship may minister the potion of imprisonment to me, in respect of poverty, but how I should be your patient to follow your prescriptions, the wise may make some dram of a scruple, or indeed a scruple itself.

Lord Chief Justice. I sent for you, when there were matters against you for your life, to come and speak with me.

Falstaff. As I was then advised by my learned counsel in the laws of this land-service, I did not come.

This adroit use of the aegis of military service to ward off the arm of the civil law was a point which inns-of-court students would take with keen amusement; but what goes before is thrust and parry of naked steel, and those who claim the scene as a triumph for Falstaff, or as proof that 'there is no gravity so firm but that he can thaw it into mirth',[49] appear to miss Shakespeare's intentions entirely. The grave face smiles at times forbearingly, no doubt; but I can see no evidence of mirth. His quibbling 'you are too impatient to bear crosses', uttered in reply to Falstaff's final fling, the pot-shot request for a loan of £1000, is sardonic pleasantry, implying that such an absurd demand is not to be taken seriously, nothing more. 'Honours easy' should, I think, be the verdict upon this first round; and in the next the fat knight gets decidedly the worst of it.

This time the scene opens with a dialogue between Mistress Quickly and sheriff's officers, bearing the pleasing names Snare and Fang, from which it appears that she is about to have Falstaff arrested for debt. Her action is prompted, we may suppose, by the prospect of his departure for York. While he continued to use her house she might hope for small payments on account—I say hope, though there is no indication in either part that Falstaff ever pays down money for anything. She could reckon also on the custom of patrons like the Prince and Poins, whom he brought with him. But all this would come to an end with his leaving for the wars, while if he were killed she could look for nothing at all. It is not our first glimpse of the shifts by which he lives. In act 3, scene 3 of Part I she complains that he owes her £24, a debt which is now

grown to over £65. Clearly he uses her as his banker, upon whom
he overdraws to an unlimited extent, without troubling her with his
newly won pension; and yet, as we have seen, his purse is empty
except for the seven groats and two pennies which the page turns
out of it in scene 2. The arrest, with the scuffle between Bardolph
and the officers, Mistress Quickly and the boy, provides plenty of
stage-fun of the horse-play variety. It shows too a Falstaff ready
for such emergencies; for no sooner does Fang pronounce the
word 'arrest' than he shouts, 'Away, varlets! Draw, Bardolph,
cut me off the villain's head, throw the quean into the channel', that
is to say, into the gutter; cries, no doubt, which often resounded
through the streets of Shakespeare's London, when catchpoles had
desperadoes to deal with. A crowd hurries up, and the situation is
just beginning to take on an ugly look, when 'Enter the Lord Chief
Justice and his men' to safeguard the King's peace; whereupon
Quickly, called upon to explain the case, proceeds to do so after
her rambling fashion.

Two facts emerge from this speech, of no relevance to her plea
but of considerable dramatic interest: first, that Prince Hal had
not long since found himself obliged to administer a thrashing to
Falstaff 'for liking his father to a singing-man of Windsor'; and
second that, while his bruises were being tended on that occasion,
Falstaff had sworn to make her his wife, borrowing thirty shillings
at the same time. Equally revealing is the defendant's reply to
these charges. 'My lord,' he explains, 'this is a poor mad soul, and
she says up and down the town that her eldest son is like you. She
hath been in good case, and the truth is, poverty hath distracted
her.' This attempt to evade the issue, and alienate the sympathies
of the Lord Chief Justice from her by suggesting that she claims
him as the father of her child, is justly stigmatized by him as
a 'more than impudent sauciness' and countered in the stern
summing-up:

You have, as it appears to me, practised upon the easy-yielding spirit
of this woman, and made her serve your uses both in purse and person.
...Pay her the debt you owe her, and unpay the villainy you have done

with her. The one you may do with sterling money, and the other with current repentance.[50]

The words are not the only hint in the play of intimate relations between Falstaff and Quickly, though (perhaps because the Folio text tones down the passage) no commentator seems to have noticed it, except Johnson, who reflects the episode in his description of Falstaff as 'always ready to cheat the weak and prey upon the poor; to terrify the timorous and insult the defenceless'.[51] Thus long before we reach Doll Tearsheet, the seamy side of Falstaff's life is being exposed to our view. It is all implicit in Hal's summary of that life at their first meeting in Part I. But we may have forgotten about such matters in the bliss of Eastcheap; and in any case express particulars are far more telling, especially upon the stage, than general statement. That they are now being brought out is an indication that Shakespeare has begun to work upon our moral sensibilities.

While Falstaff, at his lordship's appeal to him as a man of 'reputation', is patching it up with Quickly, Gower enters with letters containing more news of the King's return from Wales and of his sudden illness. After reading them, the Chief Justice questions Gower further on these grave matters. At which point, Falstaff, now disengaged, tries to thrust himself into the conversation. Three times he makes the attempt, and is ignored on each occasion by the preoccupied and anxious old statesman. Nettled at this supposed affront, he buttonholes Gower in his turn and stages a tit-for-tat by pretending to be totally deaf when the Chief Justice addresses remarks to him. It is a feeble revenge, and is dismissed by the intended victim, when he is able to grasp what it is all about, with the smiling but caustic words, 'Now the Lord lighten thee! thou art a great fool'. In the eyes of serious persons, and against a background of state affairs (which is to be the Prince's background when he becomes king), Falstaff is a very trivial sort of creature. And how absurd is Vanity, when it attempts to fence with Justice!

The tale of the 'singing-man of Windsor' is a straw that shows

the tide of our sympathies withdrawing in yet another direction.
It is idle to ask when the incident took place or to answer that, if
we go by the clock, it must have happened before the battle of
Shrewsbury. What matters is that it is mentioned now, and belongs
therefore to the atmosphere of Part II. Clearly the Prince is finding
it necessary to draw the line at familiar talk about his father's
person, and has drawn it in this instance across Falstaff's pate, which
is not surprising if we remember that 'singing-man' would in
those days probably imply eunuch. Such jesting and its reception
mark a new phase in the relations between Sir John and his young
patron; for it is difficult to imagine Falstaff indulging in similar
impudence in Part I. The nearest he comes to it is the reference, in
the play extempore, to that villainous trick of the eye and foolish
hanging of the nether lip which prove the Prince to be the very
son of his father;[52] a mere variant of the stock Elizabethan joke on
the subject of paternity, and so hardly to be taken as a reflection
upon the King himself. In Part I, indeed, it is Falstaff's cue to win
the Prince's love as well as his laughter. Phrases like 'sweet wag',
'sweet young prince', 'an thou lovest me', are constantly on his
lips; and when Hal rounds upon him for having said that he owes
him a thousand pounds, he replies: 'A thousand pound, Hal!
a million: thy love is worth a million, thou owest me thy love.'[53]
A good deal has been built upon this last. Linking it with Pistol's
word in *Henry V* of Falstaff's heart being 'fracted and corroborate',
Bradley even deduces that the fracture was caused by 'wounded
affection'.[54] Their context should have warned him that the old
humbug's professions of affection are no more to be credited than
his offers of marriage. And the true value of his love for Hal is
made evident by what he says of him behind his back in
Part II.

I have already drawn attention to Falstaff's scornful words about
him in the second scene, and noted them as part of the new swagger
he has picked up, with Hotspur's body, on the field of Shrewsbury.
At the end of the same scene he despatches his boy with letters to
various people, one to the Prince among them. The letter in ques-

tion, which comes to hand and is read aloud in act 2, scene 2,[55] has never received the attention it deserves, chiefly, I suppose, because critics have not thought of comparing it with the punctiliously ceremonious letters that have come down to us from Elizabethan times. Falstaff divides his epistle, according to the usual practice, into three parts. First, there is the superscription or address, the correct form for which may be gathered from a letter written by Ben Jonson to Cecil, which opens: 'To the most nobly-virtuous and thrice-honor'd Earle of Salisbury.'[56] That is to say, a letter should begin with the name of the addressee, accompanied by his titles and an appropriate compliment; the writer's own name being reserved till the end. Falstaff's superscription, on the other hand, which runs: 'Sir John Falstaff, knight, to the son of the king, nearest his father, Harry Prince of Wales, greeting', places the writer's name first and gives the Prince neither title nor compliment; an exceedingly impertinent proceeding, in view of the difference in rank of the two persons concerned. Poins aptly compares it with the address of a 'certificate', in other words of a licence or patent issued by a sovereign to his subject.

Nor is the epistle that follows any less saucy. The abrupt opening, 'I will imitate the honourable Romans in brevity', implies that the hero of Shrewsbury proposes to adopt the style of the victor of Zela. This he proceeds to do in the next sentence, 'I commend me to thee, I commend thee, and I leave thee', which parodies Caesar's 'veni, vidi, vici', though its meaning, 'I send you my regards, I think well of you, I am going away', is commonplace enough. After which comes this fatherly hint, 'Be not too familiar with Poins, for he misuses thy favour so much that he swears thou art to marry his sister Nell', an attempt to create prejudice almost as barefaced as the insinuations concerning Quickly that he tries to put upon the Lord Chief Justice. The scrap of spiritual advice, 'Repent at idle times as thou mayest, and so farewell', forms a suitably flippant conclusion, and is remarkable for being the only reference to repentance that Falstaff vouchsafes in Part II. Finally, we have the lofty subscription: 'Thine by yea and no, which is as much as to say, as thou usest him, Jack Falstaff with my familiars, John with my brothers and sisters, and Sir John with all Europe.'

The reading of this letter was greeted, no doubt, with shouts of laughter from all parts of the Elizabethan theatre; and it had obviously been written in the expectation that Hal and Poins would compare notes and so give the author an opportunity for another display of escape-wit.[57] Never before, however, had Falstaff gone to quite such lengths. Where is he going to stop, we ask. Is not the European reputation won at Shrewsbury proving heady wine and stimulating him to exceed the limits permitted even to an 'allowed jester'? It looks as if he is beginning to flourish his wit for its own sake, without caring whether it entertains the Prince or not. And how does his Highness take it? Will he not soon reach the point at which his descendant Victoria remarked, 'We are not amused'? There he is before us, reading the letter on the stage, and it certainly does not seem to amuse him greatly. It is from Poins that the comments on it come. All Hal says is to ask him sharply whether there is any truth in the allegation about his sister, after which he dismisses the whole business as foolery and waste of time, though partly from sheer boredom and partly with some notion of taking it out of the old ruffian, he later entertains the project of spying upon Falstaff at his assignation with Doll.

And so the scene shifts, and we find ourselves once again at the Boar's Head tavern. The famous supper-party, it will be remembered, is part of the price Quickly has to pay for the privilege of being allowed to withdraw her action for debt against Falstaff. Any ordinary blackguard would have celebrated the peace by a tête-à-tête, even if he left Madam Hostess to pay the bill. Not so Falstaff. Having taken her back into favour by borrowing an additional £10, on the security of his word as a gentleman, he gets her to seal the reconciliation by including Doll in the evening's programme, though she had been speaking only a minute or two before of his promise to make her 'my lady' his wife. It is a

palmary example of his dexterity in manipulation, and the dramatist is no less skilful in his presentation of the incident. Its sequel,
too, the second great Boar's Head scene, one of the finest instances
of Shakespeare's craftmanship in the canon, is as brilliant in its
way as the first. Yet, how different is the atmosphere! We are no
longer made to see Falstaff as 'splendid, and immortal, and desirable'; he is now the aged roué, taking his pleasures with the
dregs of the population. The note is set, first, by the character of
the jests that pass between him and his Doll, of which it is sufficient
to remark with Johnson that an interpretation 'deserves not
laborious research', and later by the Pistol episode, which develops
into a drunken brawl between a braggart and a whore.

Not that Pistol, with his head stuffed with 'play-ends' from the
old-fashioned ranting drama of the Marlowe–Peele–Greene school
of the early nineties, is anything more dangerous than a down-and-
out actor. As Falstaff remarks before he comes in: 'He's no swag-
gerer, hostess—a tame cheater. You may stroke him as gently as
a puppy greyhound. He'll not swagger with a Barbary hen, if her
feathers turn backward in any show of resistance.'[58] But he has
his lines to say, and puts on his ridiculous airs of fury when Doll
insults him, though submitting tamely enough to being chucked
out by Bardolph, who as usual does all the fighting, while Falstaff,
sword in hand, follows up at a discreet distance behind, on the
chance of getting in a thrust.[59] All the real swaggering belongs to
Doll, who does her best to work up a quarrel between the men;
such tavern-brawls, more especially when followed by bloodshed
and a kill, being meat and drink to creatures of her kind. In a later
scene, indeed, we learn that she actually manages to tarre Pistol on
to murder or manslaughter.[60] On the present occasion, however,
everything ends mildly, if laughably, enough; and though, as in
duty bound, she fondles her valorous Hector and wipes the sweat
from his 'whoreson chops', when he begins boasting that 'the
rogue fled from me like quicksilver' her disappointment and his
discretion are alike evident in the aside 'I'faith, and thou followedst
him like a church'!

At this juncture, the Prince and Poins enter disguised as potboys, to overhear Falstaff defaming their characters in the ear of the 'honest, virtuous, civil gentlewoman', and to watch the two exchanging their 'flattering busses', to say nothing of like traffic between Bardolph and the discarded Quickly. In a lecture on Tennyson, delivered in 1939 before the British Academy, Mr G. M. Young refers to what he calls 'the decorous eroticism' which hangs over much of *Idylls of the King*, and quotes the words of an American schoolboy: 'There is some pretty hot necking in Lord Tennyson, only they never quite make it.' Now, though decorous is the last word that would occur to anyone in connection with Shakespeare, this is, I believe, the only scene in his plays where 'necking', of any degree of temperature, takes place on the stage. Even Romeo is allowed to give only two kisses in view of the audience, one the 'holy kiss' at the first meeting with Juliet, in a corner of Capulet's hall, and the other the hasty farewell kiss on the ladder beneath the bedroom window. The reason is, of course, that when women's parts are taken by boy-players, passionate love-making is avoided as beyond their scope. It follows that Doll's 'necking' was intended neither to be played nor to be taken seriously. The business is introduced in order to render the fat knight still more ridiculous, and should be considered in the light of Poins's comment, 'Is it not strange that desire should so many years outlive performance?' It may even be that Doll is meant to wink at the audience as she protests 'By my troth, I kiss thee with a most constant heart'. And in inviting ridicule, does not Shakespeare also ask us for contempt? Those at any rate who pour scorn upon the spectacle of Falstaff in the last scene of *The Merry Wives*, antlered like Herne the Hunter and lisping love to Mistress Page on one side and to Mistress Ford on the other, must admit that he shows himself even more despicable on this occasion. And when the Prince and Poins, discovering themselves, tax him with defamation, he is put to his old tricks of extrication as usual; but he cringes and whines—a new note, while he is forced to have recourse to defaming Doll in turn, a shift which is neither witty nor attractive. The Boar's Head, in Part I an elysium of frolic and good fellowship, has become a brothel.

Yet the scene is, I have said, masterly in the extreme; it gives no indication whatever of either boredom of mind or slackness of hand on the part of its creator, which some critics pretend to discover. Falstaff is as sharply imagined as ever; Quickly, with her motherly concern for her young friend, is at her meandering best; and in Pistol and Doll we have two new characters which would have made the fortune of any other Elizabethan dramatist. Compare Pistol with Ben Jonson's Bobadill or Doll Tearsheet with Doll Common from the same mint, and both easily, in my judgement, hold their own. As for Mistress Tearsheet, we have, I think, to look forward to nineteenth-century French literature to find a match to this study of mingled sentimentality and brutal insentience, characteristic of the prostitute class. And is there anything, even elsewhere in Shakespeare, which exceeds the humorous tenderness and truth to nature displayed in the final moment of the scene? Let me recall it. Mars and Venus are in most awkward conjunction; for 'Now comes in the sweetest morsel of the night', and Falstaff, it seems, must hence and leave it unpicked.

Enter Bardolph

Bardolph. You must away to court, sir, presently;
    A dozen captains stay at door for you.

Falstaff [*to his Boy*]. Pay the musicians, sirrah. Farewell hostess, farewell Doll. You see, my good wenches, how men of merit are sought after. The undeserver may sleep, when a man of action is called on. Farewell, good wenches: if I be not sent away post, I will see you again ere I go.

Doll. I cannot speak: if my heart be not ready to burst.... [*sobs*] Well, sweet Jack, have a care of thyself.

Falstaff. Farewell, farewell.   [*he goes out with Bardolph.*

Hostess. Well, fare thee well. I have known thee these twenty-nine years, come peascod-time, but an honester and truer-hearted man.... [*they weep together*] Well, fare thee well.

Bardolph [*reappears at the door and calls*]. Mistress Tearsheet!

Hostess. What's the matter?

Bardolph. Bid Mistress Tearsheet come to my master.

Hostess [*kissing Doll*]. O, run Doll, run, run, good Doll.

> [*she dries Doll's face and titivates her dress.*

Bardolph [*impatient*]. Come!

Hostess. She comes blubbered!

Bardolph [*enters the room*]. Yea, will you come, Doll?

> [*he seizes her by the hand and hurries forth.*

We are not told what happens. But we may assume that Falstaff has fubbed off the dozen captains at the door, and is not seen at court before morning.

GAULTREE FOREST AND GLOUCESTERSHIRE

Once again the Old Soldier goes off to serve himself in his country's cause, and we have four rich scenes dealing with his second campaign, three of them, it is true, at Master Justice Shallow's in Gloucestershire, and only one at the scene of operations itself, and not until the battle, or rather battue, of Gaultree Forest is over. We shall not need to follow him through these scenes as closely as we have followed him hitherto, since they raise no fresh difficulties. I propose, therefore, to pass them over with a few general observations.

They show us, in the first place, the fortunes of Falstaff, after the temporary and, on the surface, unimportant check of his exposure by the Prince, rising steadily until they reach their zenith in that culmination of all his dreams, the news of the old King's death. The luck of Shrewsbury follows him to Gaultree; for so terrible has his name grown to the enemy that 'a famous rebel' Sir John Colevile surrenders to him at discretion. Thus his military reputation is still further enhanced, without the shedding of one drop of sweat, and he is furnished with a complete reply to Prince John's complaint of his tardy appearance. At the same time, Shakespeare recaptures for us something of pristine glory with which Falstaff gladdened our spirits in Part I. Never, for instance, is he more serenely brilliant, even when discoursing upon Honour before the battle of Shrewsbury, than in the great speech, which sober-blooded Prince John provokes, on the properties of sack, a speech that is an Elizabethan treatise on psychology in little. In the Gloucestershire scenes too all is gaiety and good humour. Here there is no danger of running into the Lord Chief Justice, of being clapped on the shoulder by Mistress Quickly's nuthooks, of tiresome passages with yea-forsooth tradesmen, who stand upon security. In a word, the troubles of the capital are a hundred miles and more behind him; he has the profitable business in hand of taking up soldiers as he goes north; and a still richer prize is in prospect; for an old dotard, possessor of land and beefs, is proud to claim an ancient acquaintance with a soldier grown so great, and, given a little tempering, that is to say a little warming up with draughts of sack and promises of court favour, may be persuaded to seal to any sum at request. *Et in Arcadia ipse!*

It is an odd fact that many romantic critics, who can swallow nearly all Falstaff's actions in Part II, and even pass lightly over his treatment of Mistress Quickly, find the manipulation of Shallow stick in their throats. Morgann describes it as 'abominably dissolute', declares that it 'creates disgust', and presumes 'that Shakespeare meant to connect this fraud with the punishment of Falstaff, as a...ground of censure and dishonour'.[61] I cannot believe that Shakespeare intended us to contemplate the over-reaching of Shallow with anything but tolerant amusement; still less that a London audience would do so at the end of the sixteenth century; especially if, as seems likely, a fair proportion of them consisted of inns-of-court men. The household of Shallow, with its pitiful peasantry lined up in the first scene for Falstaff's inspection, and ours; with Davy, its man-of-all-work, who acts as serving-man, husbandman, and justice's clerk, turn and turn about, and is even prepared to assume the part of host, when his master's eyes are a little sunk in's head; above all with its brace of witless country justices, is a studied burlesque of provincial life and manners for the hilarious contempt of London spectators. One point is of itself sufficient to prove this: the youthful escapades which Shallow recounts with such complacent satisfaction, unconscious that with every boast he reveals himself the laughing-stock of his former companions, are all placed in London, where he is represented as a law student of one of the inferior 'inns' fifty to fifty-five years before. Shakespeare brings in Justice Shallow, not to fill the cup of Falstaff's iniquity to the brim, but to give him 'easy meat' and so deepen our impression of the tide running strongly in his favour. Not that we imagine he can escape the fate that awaits him. But just as 'a lightning before death' in the hero belongs to the technique of Shakespearian tragedy, so in comedy a quickened sense of opportunity and security on the part of the knave or intriguer, shortly before his final discomfiture, adds much to the enjoyment of the audience.

The diversions of Gloucestershire, at first sight a mere dramatic digression, serve other purposes also. Master Justice Shallow and his cousin Silence in commission with him have their place in the symbolic scheme, inasmuch as they offset the majesty and native dignity of the Lord Chief Justice. And the fact that Falstaff extracts from them the £1000 he fails to borrow from his lordship serves to underline the contrast. Foiled in his attempts to thrust the latter from a level consideration, Falstaff finds in these provincial representatives of 'old father antic the Law', mannikins whose motions he can control like a couple of puppets. And not he only. The servant Davy, pleading with Shallow on behalf of a friend, whose case is to come up at the next quarter sessions and who is well known as an arrant knave, protests: 'I have served your worship truly, sir, this eight years, and if I cannot *once or twice in a quarter* bear out a knave against an honest man, I have but a very little credit with your worship.'[62] The truth is that Justices of the Peace, consequential representatives of the Privy Council, were considered unsatisfactory instruments of the Law in aristocratic circles at the end of the sixteenth century, and Shakespeare is not the only dramatist to give expression to these sentiments.[63] Shallow and Silence act as foils, moreover, not only to the Chief Justice but also to Falstaff himself. Not since Holofernes and Parson Nathaniel walked together on to the stage in *Love's Labour's Lost* had Shakespeare introduced two such egregious scarecrows as he does with the entry of the worshipful cousins at the beginning of act 3, scene 2. Herford describes their opening dialogue as 'a masterpiece of the humour which comes from talk studiously denuded of all conscious humorous suggestion';[64] and insipidity of speech is matched with bodies so forlorn that their dimensions to any thick sight are invisible, and so sapless that they seem like little figures of men made, after supper, of cheeseparings. Thus when, after eighty lines of all this, Falstaff himself comes in, his fatness and his wit appear twice blessed. And yet, such is the genius of their creator, the creatures live! When, warmed with a little sack, Cousin Silence bursts into song and Falstaff encouragingly remarks, 'I did not think Master Silence had been a man of this mettle', the reply, 'Who I? I have been merry twice and once ere now',[65] could only have come from human lips breathing a human spirit, starved though it be.

Lastly, and perhaps chiefly, Shakespeare needed Shallow for his final scene. This is shown, I think, by his withholding from us the little matter of the £1000 loan until then. It does not come upon us quite without notice, because Falstaff has told us more than once that he has marked down his prey. But the loan and its amount are first casually mentioned when the two take up their position together at the door of the Abbey. Thus our minds are given just enough time to assimilate the idea before it is reiterated with tremendous effect immediately after the rejection. In short, Shallow serves both to set the fat knight off, and to support him, most unwillingly it is true, in his hour of disaster. But I am anticipating.

CHAPTER VI

THE CHOICE AND THE BALANCE

It has been convenient to consider Hal and Falstaff separately in the last two chapters; and as they seldom meet in Part II, the method would seem an innocuous one. Yet any departure from the dramatic order of presentation has its pitfalls, and by this sorting out of scenes under different headings, we fail to take account of the light that each scene derives from the scene before it, or sheds in turn upon the scene that comes after. I can claim in extenuation that often, and for most of Part II, there is little more than a change from grave to gay or *vice versa*, as the scene shifts to and fro between Falstaff and Westminster, Master Shallow's and the opposing camps in the field, and that what is lost in dramatic value through the separate treatment of the two characters—and loss there certainly has been—are impressions which would be found, I think, to tell in favour of the general argument of this book rather than the reverse. Certainly, as we draw near the end of the play, the alternation of scenes becomes increasingly significant; is indeed, as all who have seen Part II on the stage can testify, one of Shakespeare's principal means of working upon the imagination of his audience; operating as it does like a succession of hammer-strokes, now from one side, now from the other, to drive home the inevitability, the justice, of the choice Hal is about to make. In dealing, therefore, with the skilfully disposed fifth act, which forms the subject of this final chapter, I propose to follow the play scene by scene.

COMIC COUNTERPOINT

We pass into Gloucestershire at the beginning of it straight from the side of the dying King's couch, from the sight of the Prince kneeling to make his vows and from the tender reconciliation between father and son. After all this Falstaff, just arrived at Shallow's house from Yorkshire, brings comic relief. The more so that, as we know from act 4, scene 3, the object of his visit is to thrust his hand deep into the J.P.'s pocket, while the old dotard on his side is laying himself out to entertain his guests, despite their 'marvellous foul linen', in order to secure a powerful friend at court. It is a situation amusing in itself which also points us forward to the end of the play. The most skilful and suggestive piece of pointing, however, is the soliloquy with which Falstaff concludes the scene. After holding Shallow and his servants up to ridicule, he goes on:

> I will devise matter enough out of this Shallow to keep Prince Harry in continual laughter the wearing out of six fashions—which is four terms, or two actions—and a' shall laugh without intervallums. O, it is much that a lie with a slight oath, and a jest with a sad brow, will do with a fellow that never had the ache in his shoulders! O, you shall see him laugh till his face be like a wet cloak ill laid up.[1]

By itself this is little more than a characteristic piece of comic arrogance. But it is not by itself. As noted above, it is heard by spectators who have also just heard Prince Harry's solemn self-dedication and words of passionate affection, who have seen his face stained with the tears, not of laughter, but of grief. That, they must feel, is a Harry impossible for Falstaff even to imagine, while the hold he speaks of with such confidence is not upon the Prince at all, but upon a piece of masquing stuff that, as they know, the Prince has doffed for ever.

Nor is this all. His scornful talk of a likeness between Shallow and his servants, a likeness which grows daily closer because 'they by observing of him do bear themselves like foolish justices; he by conversing with them is turned into a justice-like serving man', concludes with the following aphorism:

> It is certain that either wise bearing or ignorant carriage is caught, as men take diseases, one of another: therefore, let men take heed of their company.

Heard with the rest of his patter, the sentence passes almost unnoticed. Isolated, it seems more appropriate to the lips of Polonius than to those of Falstaff. Why did Shakespeare give him this little sermon, so utterly out of character? For the same reason that in *Hamlet* he makes the Player King expatiate on the theme of Will and Fate or King Claudius condemn Procrastination:[2] unobtrusively to remind us, that is, of the main theme of the play, to whisper as it were in our ears a variant of the Pauline 'Evil communications corrupt good manners'; in a word, to point us on to the end. That we are hardly conscious of the suggestion, that it is actually placed in the mouth of the evil companion himself, makes no matter; it is but a touch of the brush, and is added to the canvas not to attract attention—on the contrary—but to contribute to the total effect. What we *are* conscious of is the shallowness of this contemner of Shallow; and having heard him declare how easy it is to fool a young fool like Hal, we are immediately switched over to the Presence Chamber at Westminster, to see Hal himself; now, by the death of his father, King Henry V.

But first of all it is made obvious that everyone at court believes the new reign will bring disaster to England. Even the royal brothers fear the worst, while the Lord Chief Justice, having formerly committed the Prince of Wales to prison, has no hope either for the realm or of pardon for himself, and is steeling his resolution to follow his 'master that is dead'. Forty lines of this form an effective prologue to the entry of the young King himself, and the exhibition of a spirit entirely different from anything the speakers expect. He utters gracious and encouraging words to his brothers, remarking with something of a twinkle in his eye,

> This is the English not the Turkish court,
> Not Amurath an Amurath succeeds,
> But Harry Harry.

Then he turns to the Chief Justice, and the second half of the scene is devoted to the reconciliation between them, which consists of the old man's defence of his past conduct, nobly combining respect for the King's majesty and a stout adherence to the doctrine of the Rule of Law, and of the young King's equally noble reply, in which the courtesy and humility that had marked his words and deeds on the field of honour at Shrewsbury are now displayed as notably in the sphere of civil Justice. The story of the wild prince boxing the Lord Chief Justice's ears as he sat on the judgement-seat may be pure legend, and the scene of reconciliation the invention of poetic imagination; yet the speeches just mentioned so well express the best thought of the age on the relations between the crown and its representatives on the bench that they deserve quotation among documents of the British constitution. Of special note from the dramatic point of view are the lines of the Prince:

> There is my hand.
> You shall be as a father to my youth,
> My voice shall sound as you do prompt mine ear,
> And I will stoop and humble my intents
> To your well-practised, wise directions.

He has found a friend and a counsellor and a father at last; and he promises to be guided in all things by his advice. What chance has Falstaff with such a Prince? The young man has already made his choice between Justice and Vanity. The fat knight is rejected before he can have sight of his sweet boy.

Unconscious that his fate is being thus sealed, Falstaff, to whom we now return, is still busy at Justice Shallow's, drinking with him and his brilliant cousin Master Silence. In the midst of a tipsy carouse, in which Sir John's rolling sphere is well set off by a tottering spindleshanks on either hand, Pistol arrives with tidings of the old King's death. At once Falstaff is all sobriety, determination, and overweening self-confidence.

Master Shallow, my Lord Shallow—be what thou wilt, I am Fortune's steward—get on thy boots, we'll ride all night.... Boot, boot, Master Shallow! I know the young king is sick for me. Let us take any man's horses; the laws of England are at my commandment. Blessed are they that have been my friends, and woe to my Lord Chief Justice![3]

To an audience which has just watched the Prince adopting my Lord Chief Justice as his father, these last words will appear crazily self-assured. And what is the rest but Falstaff's version of the vision of the rule of Riot in England which had haunted the mind of the dying King? As if to drive the point well home, the character of this rule is vividly shown in the scene that follows. The dreadful Doll, harridan and whore, is being dragged off with Quickly to Bridewell to be whipped by beadles for beating a man to death with the help of Pistol, the latter having evidently escaped arrest himself by his journey into Gloucestershire. The groundlings, no doubt, enjoyed the episode with much laughter; but it is gruesome-grotesque, displaying the ugliest side of Eastcheap life, and deliberately introduced at this point of the play to throw the last weight into the scales against Falstaff before the moment of his open rejection.

SIR JOHN AT THE FLEET

In considering that moment itself, several misunderstandings have to be cleared up. In the first place, a false interpretation has been placed upon the committal by the Lord Chief Justice of Falstaff and his company to the Fleet. Bradley, who finds this particularly objectionable, speaks of 'the strange incident of the Chief Justice being sent back to order Falstaff to prison' and suggests that the young King 'after he had left Falstaff and was no longer influenced by the face of his old companion...gave way to anger at the indecent familiarity which had provoked a compromising scene on the most ceremonial of occasions and in the presence alike of court and crowd, and had sent the Chief Justice back to take vengeance'.[4] But the arrest is no afterthought. Bradley forgets that at the end of his speech to Falstaff the King expressly charges the Lord Chief Justice

To see performed the tenour of our word,

so that, after the procession has passed on, the judge returns with officers to lay the whole party by the heels pending the examination the King had ordered.

Nor is there the least hint of vengeance, or even of sending Falstaff to prison in the ordinary sense of the word. With the abolition of the Star Chamber in 1641 the Fleet lost its former character, became a squalid debtors' prison, and remained so until 1846, which explains why Dr Johnson himself was puzzled by the reference to it in 2 *Henry IV*. An Elizabethan audience would find nothing puzzling. To them the Fleet was a prison of a special and superior kind, used by the Privy Council, as well as by other government courts or officials, for the temporary custody of persons summoned before them for enquiry, whom they could not at the moment deal with. The highest in the land might be treated in this way, which, though no doubt irksome, was not considered much of a hardship and certainly not a disgrace.[5] As the editor of *Henry IV* in 'The Arden Shakespeare', who seems to have been the first to set the matter in its true light, has well said:

> Falstaff's ultimate disgrace and punishment have gained for him much undeserved commiseration; the punishment to which he is condemned—temporary imprisonment in the Fleet and banishment from court—was not exceptionally severe. Queen Elizabeth inflicted similar sentences upon favourite courtiers and court ladies who incurred her displeasure. To Shakespeare's contemporaries the King's treatment of Falstaff would not appear harsh; imprisonment in the Fleet involved discomfort but not dishonour.[6]

Nothing more than a brief detention is implied by the context. To Falstaff's protesting 'My lord, my lord—' when the officers lay hands upon him, the Chief Justice replies:

> I cannot now speak, I will hear you *soon*;

which suggests an examination in a few hours' time or perhaps next day; and after that, release would presumably follow. A lengthy imprisonment, in any event, is incompatible with the sentence of banishment to a distance of at least ten miles from Westminster. Clearly, we are expected to imagine Falstaff under lock and key during the coronation festivities, but no longer. His committal to the Fleet is even something of a compliment: it implies that he is a person of distinction.

KING HENRY'S SPEECH

If my readers have followed me to this point they will, I think, be prepared to agree that the rejection has become inevitable. Ought we, nevertheless, to resent with Bradley the manner in which it is carried out? My reply is that what he calls the 'sermon'[7] is in keeping at once with Hal's character and with his situation, and not only dramatically effective but probably the only effective way of terminating the play which Shakespeare could have devised. Let readers and spectators put themselves first in the young King's place, and then in his creator's, and ask themselves what else either could have done in the circumstances. Having watched him kneeling at his father's death-bed and heard him making his noble peace with the Lord Chief Justice, we can be certain, and should be fully aware, that at this moment, with the crown of England newly placed upon his head, the chrism still glistening upon his forehead, and his spirit uplifted by one of the most solemn acts of dedication and consecration which the Christian Church has to offer, all his thoughts and emotions will be concentrated upon the great task to which he has been called, its duties and responsibilities. It is a fatal moment for Falstaff to present himself. Even Bradley admits that the rogue now behaves 'in so fatuous and outrageous a manner that great sternness on the King's part was unavoidable'.[8] May we not go farther and say that anger would be both natural and excusable to anyone in such a mood, more especially to one who, 'being incensed', is 'flint'?[9]

The job had to be done, a clean cut made; and on every count it had to be made publicly. Bradley contradicts himself, in effect, by suggesting on the one hand that Hal should have communicated his decision to Falstaff 'in a private interview rich in humour and merely touched with pathos', and, by complaining on the other hand, that 'Shakespeare has so contrived matters' that no such 'private warning' is possible.[10] The truth is surely that Shakespeare very well knew that any talk of a private nature between Hal and Falstaff at this juncture would be too difficult even for his powers. It is not that Harry, as some hold, would find the double pull of old affections and improvised brilliance, as always, quite irresistible, but that Shakespeare himself has been busy ever since Shrewsbury manœuvring these former friends into different universes between which conversation is impossible. And if the language of the speech sounds formal and homiletic, that is because Hal is learning to speak, not as Bradley complains 'like a clergyman',[11] but like the Chief Justice, to whom he had just promised that his voice should sound as he did prompt his ear. The adoption of the Justice as his father and the consecration at the Abbey had completed the process of separation, and the only speech the regenerate Harry can now have with his old Adam is a public one.

Not that he relishes the task or finds it easy. When Falstaff first confronts him, and that great red face breaks in upon his 'white celestial thought', he tries to avoid the encounter, begging the Lord Chief Justice to say for him what must be said. But Falstaff, on fire with anticipation, brushes the old judge aside, so that there is nothing for it: the King must speak the unpleasant words himself. And just because they have to be unpleasant, unpleasant to himself as well as to the man he addresses, to say nothing of the publicity and the fact that his brothers, the court and the Chief Justice stand there listening how he will comport himself after his recent announcement of reformation, will he not be on his mettle and perhaps use language blunter and harsher than he might otherwise have done? Even so, he falters and finds it difficult to keep it up. For, as Warburton has shrewdly observed, having used the word 'gormandizing' by chance, and

that word unluckily presenting him with a pleasant idea, he cannot forbear pursuing it—

> Know the grave doth gape
> For thee thrice wider than for other men—

and is just falling back into Hal, by a humorous allusion to Falstaff's bulk; but he perceives it immediately, and fearing Sir John should take the advantage of it, checks both himself and the knight, with—

> Reply not to me with a fool-born jest;

and so resumes the thread of his discourse.[12]

As for

> 'I know thee not, old man. Fall to thy prayers,

and the rest of it, while such sentiments may be harsh, to call them 'ungenerous' is to misapprehend the relationship between the knight and his patron, and to call them 'dishonest' is even more absurd. The terms are again Bradley's, who goes so far as to stigmatize the speech as 'an attempt to buy the praise of the respectable at the cost of honour and truth'.[13] Charges of this kind would never, I think, have occurred to a critic before the end of the nineteenth century. Respectability, the word and the social quality, were of mid-eighteenth century origin, and did not even begin to fall into disfavour until at least a hundred years later; about which time the phenomenon of conversion, of which the change in Henry Monmouth is an instance, also ceased to be regarded as normal or desirable by average serious-minded persons. King Henry V is a new man; he had buried his 'wildness' in his father's grave; he speaks as the representative and embodiment of

> The majesty and power of law and justice.[14]

I cannot believe that members of an Elizabethan audience would have felt the 'sermon' anything but fine and appropriate. And if some, as Rowe suggests, may have 'in remembrance of the diversion' Falstaff 'had formerly afforded 'em, been sorry to see his friend Hal use him so scurvily',[15] others would assuredly have retorted with Johnson:

> but if it be considered that the fat knight has never uttered one sentiment of generosity, and with all his power of exciting mirth, has nothing in him that can be esteemed, no great pain will be suffered from the reflection that he is compelled to live honestly, and maintained by the King, with a promise of advancement when he shall deserve it.[16]

As for ourselves, how characteristically muddle-headed it is that a generation which has almost universally condemned a prince of its own for putting private inclinations before his public obligations, should condemn Hal as a cad and a prig for doing just the opposite.

But more important than all these questions of moral decorum, which are the plague of modern dramatic criticism, are those of dramatic decorum, in which critics of a former age took greater interest. And here, at any rate, there can be no question of the rightness of Shakespeare's finale. Preparing his audience for the rejection from the beginning, and making it appear ever more inevitable the nearer he approaches to it, in the end he springs it upon them in the most striking and unexpected fashion possible. Under the conditions of stage-performance, the only conditions which Shakespeare contemplated, both the encounter outside the Abbey and the speech of the King are extraordinarily effective.

THE HEART 'FRACTED AND CORROBORATE'

At this point some of my readers will exclaim: But it is not the end; you have forgotten the death-bed scene as depicted by Mistress Quickly in *Henry V*, and Pistol's testimony that the man dies of a broken heart.[17] I have already pointed out in my first chapter that what happens or is said in *Henry V* has no dramatic relevance to the events in *Henry IV*. But, lest anyone should think that this is to brush aside too lightly what many consider one of the gravest charges in the indictment against Harry Monmouth, a word or two more may be said about it here. Certainly, Bradley regards it very seriously. Following up a characteristic effusion by Swinburne,[18] he writes: 'Falstaff's dismissal to the Fleet, and his subsequent death, prove beyond doubt that his rejection was meant by Shakespeare to be taken as a catastrophe which not even his humour could enable him to surmount.'[19] We have seen that he is wrong on the first count, the Epilogue to Part II proves him equally wrong on the second. 'One word more,' its last clause begins, 'if you be not too much cloyed with fat meat, our humble author will continue the story, with Sir John in it, and make you merry with fair Katherine of France; where, for anything I know, Falstaff shall die of a sweat, unless already a' be killed with your hard opinions; for Oldcastle died a martyr, and this is not the man.' If words and the tone of words mean anything at all, the last thing Shakespeare had in mind when he wrote these was a sad death for his fat knight. On the contrary, as he concluded *Henry IV*, his intention was to make use of the old soldier in yet a third campaign, that of Agincourt, where he would once again 'sweat to death and lard the lean earth', this time of France and not Kent. And the intention, thus publicly announced, amounted to a promise and an advertisement of future delights to an audience whose appetite for such 'fat meat', if the contemporary records of Falstaff's popularity go for anything, so far from being cloyed, had at the end of two plays only grown by what it fed on.

Why the promise was not, or could not be, fulfilled we do not know. Dr Johnson supposed, as I have already stated, that when it came to the point Shakespeare found it difficult to contrive the projected continuation in dramatic terms, and was forced to abandon it. My own guess, which follows a suggestion of Professor H. D. Gray,[20] is that the suppression of Falstaff in *Henry V* was due, not to failure of invention on the part of Shakespeare, but to changes in the personnel of his acting company. We know very little about the casting of Shakespeare's plays, but William Kempe was the comic man of the Lord Chamberlain's men, one of the principal sharers, and very popular with the London public; so that it seems natural to assume that the character of Falstaff was written for and, theatrically speaking, created by him. The Quarto of Part II even has a stage-direction, 'Enter Will', early in the Doll scene (2. 4) which is paralleled by 'Enter Will Kemp' in the Second Quarto of *Romeo and Juliet* and is best explained, I think, as a Falstaff entry for the same player.[21] Certainly the hypothesis that Kempe played Falstaff in the original productions of *Henry IV*, which belong to the years 1597-98, offers a neat and satisfactory answer to the question why Shakespeare did not keep faith with his public. The reference in the Chorus of the fifth act of *Henry V* to the expedition, under the Earl of Essex, for the subjugation of Ireland, ties the first performances of that play to the period between 27 March and 28 September 1599, at which dates the unfortunate young man left England and returned. Whether the reference to 'this wooden O' in the opening Chorus glances at the Globe or the Curtain playhouse as the place of production is uncertain. What is certain is that the building of the Globe was taken in hand early in 1599 and completed sometime in the summer, that the legal document about the lease of its site on Bankside signed 21 February includes the name of William Kempe among the lessees, and that he withdrew from the enterprise 'about the time of the building...or shortly after',[22] while we have evidence of other kinds that he left the company in that year. The theory, in short, is that when Shakespeare promised, in the Epilogue to *Henry IV*, a Falstaff in *Henry V* he contemplated that Kempe would be there to play him, but that, Kempe having left in the meantime, he was obliged to alter his plans. And if Falstaff could not appear, a dramatic explanation for his absence must be provided, and the only satisfactory one was an account of his death. Accordingly we get the picture of his end, shot with that blend of pathos and humour of which Shakespeare was master, and in the writing of which he put forth his full powers in an endeavour to win indulgence from the spectators for the disappointment of their hopes.

But if that Falstaff dies a martyr to the King's unkindness, he is not the man we see in *Henry IV*. For what the commiserators of Falstaff appear to overlook is that the delicious old sinner has no need of their pity. Shakespeare does not dismiss him in silence and with bowed head;[23] he gives him his word, and a later word than the King's. It is a word too in which we see the dramatist holding, as ever, his balance even. We have applauded Majesty turning from Vanity in his hour of consecration towards the austere path of law and government; we have now to admire the demeanour of the Tempter thus suddenly cast down from the very gate of Heaven. The scene, indeed, affords not the slightest indication of that fat heart being 'fracted and corroborate'. On the contrary, never does it give clearer proof of stout intrepidity, not even when the sheriff in Part I interrupts the interlude at the Boar's Head. As a German critic pointed out long ago,[24] instead of replying to his royal Hal with reproachful reminders of past friendship, he counts his blessings and rejoices, like Milton's Satan, that 'all is not lost'. 'Master Shallow,' he remarks with a wicked smile to the chap-fallen justice at his side, when the procession has swept on, 'I owe you a thousand pound!' He had dreamed of that thousand ever since it was taken and retaken on Gad's Hill;[25] he had made out that Hal was indebted to him for it; he had actually on one occasion tried to borrow it from the Lord Chief Justice himself. And now he has lifted it from the pocket of an old father antic in Gloucestershire and has it safe in his own, let Hal rave and storm as he will at his iniquities. Nor is this sheer effrontery. There is method in it. No sooner does he realize that his credit with the King is bankrupt than his eager intellect is busily at work trying to brazen it out with those in his party. 'I shall be sent for in private to him, look you,' he assures them; 'he must seem thus to the world: fear not your advancements—I will be the man yet that shall make you great.' And when his old enemies Fang and Snare, who turn up again in the train of the Chief Justice, close in upon him, his protesting shouts, 'My lord, my lord', tell us that a 'confident brow' is his to the very end and that 'the throng of words that come with such more than impudent sauciness from him is only cut short because he is hustled out of earshot on his way to the Fleet.

SHAKESPEARE'S BALANCE

Thus, though Shakespeare's Prince rejects Falstaff, and Shakespeare shows the rejection to be both right and necessary, Falstaff is never rejected by Shakespeare himself as some suppose.[26] On the contrary, we are sent away with the assurance that full and ample provision has been made for his future. The King promises a 'competence of life', and this is enlarged upon by Prince John, who is presumably in the know and, what is dramatically more important, with whose words we take our final leave of Falstaff in the play:

> I like this fair proceeding of the King's:
> He hath intent his wonted followers
> Shall all be *very well provided for*.

Let us not forget either that in addition to this allowance from the privy purse, there is Justice Shallow's £1000, not a penny of which will ever see Gloucestershire again. Of course, we know that the purse of the old ruffian himself is subject to an incurable consumption which no royal pension or borrowing from country justices can do anything but linger out. But that, like the circumference of his belly, is a mere condition of his existence, independent both of the smiles of Fortune and the favour of princes. Enough for us that 'we end the play with the delightful feeling that while Henry has done the right thing' by England, himself, and his former companions, 'Falstaff in his outward overthrow has still proved himself inwardly invincible'.[27]

The feeling is something more than delightful: it is just. Shakespeare sends us home happy, but neither hoodwinked nor duped, as our theatrical entertainers too often dismiss us. We are not to imagine that, because kings should be virtuous and society needs a framework of decency, order, and justice to hold it together, there shall be no more cakes and ale, or that ginger will cease to be hot in the mouths of succeeding generations of men. Indeed, the progressive organization of the world during the last three centuries, which has caused the claims of social and political obligation to become ever more insistent and compelling, has also by reaction caused the invincibility of Falstaff to seem increasingly precious and significant. In a little book on Shakespeare published some years ago I suggested that Falstaff, for all his descent from a medieval devil, has become a kind of god in the mythology of modern man, a god who does for our imaginations very much what Bacchus or Silenus did for those of the ancients; and this because we find it extraordinarily exhilarating to contemplate a being free of all the conventions, codes and moral ties that control us as members of human society, a being without shame, without principles, without even a sense of decency, and yet one who manages to win our admiration by his superb wit, his moral effrontery, his intellectual agility, and his boundless physical vitality.[28]

Yet the English spirit has ever needed two wings for its flight, Order as well as Liberty; and in none of Shakespeare's plays is the English spirit more explicit, or more completely expressed, than in *Henry IV*. The play celebrates a double coronation, that of our English Bacchus who, with the sprig of rue in his garland, reigns for ever from his state at the Boar's Head, and that of English Harry, in whose person Shakespeare crowns *noblesse oblige*, generosity and magnanimity, respect for law, and the selfless devotion to duty which comprise the traditional ideals of our public service. This balance which the play keeps between the bliss of freedom and the claims of the common weal has been disturbed by modern critics through a failure to preserve a similar balance in themselves. For what Lascelles Abercrombie called our liberty of interpreting Shakespeare[29] must be constantly checked and reinspired by the discipline of Shakespearian scholarship. In the foregoing attempt to discover Shakespeare's intentions and to recapture glimpses of the vision which this widest of all his dramatic horizons opened up to the Elizabethan public, both in the popular playhouse and at court, I have endeavoured to do something to readjust the balance. In effect, it has meant trying to put Falstaff in his place, his place within the frame of the drama from which Morgann and his successors, to the confusion of criticism, had inadvisedly released him. I offer no apologies for constraining the old boar to feed in the old frank: for it is a spacious pinfold, with room and to spare for even the greatest of comic creations.

NOTES

References to the text of Shakespeare follow the line-enumeration of 'The New Shakespeare', that of 'The Globe Shakespeare' being added in brackets, where the two differ.

I. BACK TO JOHNSON

1. A lesser critic who has seen the play steadily and seen it whole is the American, H. N. Hudson. His *Shakespeare: his Life, Art, Characters*, 2 vols. 1872 is an interesting blend of sound critical perception and 'early Victorian' moralizing. It is also tiresomely arranged, which probably accounts for the comparative and undeserved neglect into which it has fallen, even among the writer's fellow-countrymen. It should be noted that, like Johnson, Hudson knew his Shakespeare as an editor. The same may be said of K. Deighton, editor of the useful school texts of Shakespeare in Macmillan's 'English Classics', who is a follower of Hudson and writes sensibly of Falstaff and Hal. That the editor of both parts of *Henry IV* in 'The Arden Shakespeare' cannot be classed with these is due, I expect, to the fact that his editorial experience was confined to this play, so that he never came, for all his learning, quite to understand what drama means. Among critics at large, Kreyssig, Dowden (who follows Hudson, more than is commonly realized), and Brandes have all just things to say about Prince Hal: but none attempts a dramatic appraisement of the play as a whole. Nor indeed does a little book on Shakespeare, published in 1929, by John Bailey, which contains nevertheless the sanest comments since Johnson's. In writing my book how often have I found what seemed to me a fresh point of view already stated in the few pages he was able to spare for *Henry IV* (cf. note 16 below)! Johnson, Hudson and Bailey, taken together, will be found to anticipate a good deal of what follows.

2. Elmer Edgar Stoll, *Shakespeare Studies*, 1927, p. 409.

3. J. Dover Wilson, *What happens in 'Hamlet'*, 1935, pp. 94, 202, 229.

4. Johnson's *Shakespeare*, 1765, iv, p. 235.

5. C. F. Tucker Brooke, *Tudor Drama*, 1911, p. 333.

6. Stoll, *op. cit.* pp. 455–6. This revealing paragraph is virtually an admission that, on Prof. Stoll's reading of Falstaff's character, there

is no real difference between the Falstaffs of *Henry IV* and *The Merry Wives*.

7. Johnson, *op. cit.* iv, p. 397.

8. Oliver Elton, *A Survey of English Literature, 1780–1830*, ii, p. 361.

9. Masefield, *Shakespeare* ('Home University Library'), 1911, pp. 112–13; cf. H. B. Charlton, *Shakespearean Comedy*, 1938, pp. 165–6.

10. Bradley, *Oxford Lectures*, 1909, p. 257.

11. Masefield, *op. cit.* p. 113.

12. Charlton, *op. cit.* p. 169 *et passim*.

13. A. C. Swinburne, *A Study of Shakespeare*, 1880, p. 115.

14. Johnson, *op. cit.* iv, pp. 355–6.

15. Maurice Morgann, *Essay on the Dramatic Character of Sir John Falstaff*, 1777, ed. by W. A. Gill, 1912, pp. 58–62 (footnote). Morgann's best things are in his footnotes, and are obviously generalizations that flashed upon him as he followed up the particular arguments in the text.

16. John Bailey, *A Note on Falstaff*, pp. 149–52 of *A Book of Homage to Shakespeare*, ed. by Israel Gollancz, 1916. Bailey's debt to Johnson is evident in his little book on Shakespeare, *v. infra*, ch. III, note 3, while his volume on Johnson in 'The Home University Library' is one of the best of all popular expositions.

17. Bradley, *op. cit.* p. 259.   18. Charlton, *op. cit.* p. 171.

19. Bradley, *op. cit.* pp. 261–2.   20. Johnson, *op. cit.* iv, p. 356.

21. Cf. Quiller-Couch, *Shakespeare's Workmanship*, p. 152: 'Johnson could not help loving Falstaff. They were both men of extravagant bulk, too, and both good Londoners.'

22. Cf. Raleigh, *Shakespeare* ('English Men of Letters'), p. 189: 'He [Falstaff] is never for a moment entangled in the net of his own deceits, his mind is absolutely clear of cant; his self-respect is magnificent and unfailing.' But cf. pp. 93 ff.

23. The weak spot in Johnson's criticism of *Henry IV* is his condemnation of Pt. II, act 5 as a 'lame and impotent conclusion'. Cf. *infra*, ch. VI.

II. THE FALSTAFF MYTH

1. I refer to 3.1 of Pt. I, which was headed 'The Archbishop of Bangor's House in Wales' by Theobald and later editors, though without any warrant in Shakespeare. Glendower behaves like a host throughout the scene, which is clearly a family party.

2. *V.* Alfred Ainger, *Lectures and Essays*, 1905, i, pp. 140–55.

3. In what follows I develop a hint in Sir Arthur Quiller-Couch's *Shakespeare's Workmanship*, 1918, p. 148: 'The whole of the business [in *Henry IV*] is built on the old Morality structure, imported through the Interlude. Why, it might almost be labelled, after the style of a Morality title, *Contentio inter Virtutem et Vitium de anima Principis*.'

4. *The enterlude of youth*, ed. by W. Bang and R. B. McKerrow, Louvain, 1905.

5. riot='wanton, loose, or wasteful living; debauchery, dissipation, extravagance' (*O.E.D.*). Cf. the Prodigal Son, who 'wasted his substance with riotous living' (Luke xv. 13).

6. *V.* C. H. Herford, *The Literary Relations between England and Germany in the Sixteenth Century*, 1886, ch. III, pp. 84–95.

7. Pt. I, 2. 4. 450 (508); cf. l. 435 (491): 'Thou art violently carried away from grace, there is a devil haunts thee in the likeness of an old fat man.'

8. *Ibid.* 2. 4. 442 (500).   9. Pt. II, 5. 5. 63 (66).

10. Cf. Pt. I, 1. 1. 85: 'Riot and dishonour stain the brow / Of my young Harry'; Pt. II, 4. 4. 62: 'His headstrong riot hath no curb', 4. 5. 135: 'When that my care could not withhold thy riots, / What wilt thou do when riot is thy care?'

11. In particular, the exact significance of the Vice is exasperatingly obscure. Cf. the discussion by Sir E. K. Chambers (*Medieval Stage*, ii, pp. 203–5), who concludes 'that whatever the name may mean...the character of the vice is derived from that of the domestic fool or jester'. I hazard the suggestion that it was originally the title or name of the Fool who attended upon the Lord of Misrule; *v.* Feuillerat, *Revels of the time of Edward VI*, p. 73: 'One vyces dagger & a ladle with a bable pendante...deliuerid to the Lorde of Mysrules foole.'

12. Fabyan's *Chronicle*, 1516, p. 577.

13. C. L. Kingsford, *The First English Life of King Henry the Fifth*, 1911, pp. xlii, xliii.

14. *V.* pp. xvi–xix, lviii–lix of my Introd. to *Richard II*, 1939 ('The New Shakespeare').   15. Kingsford, *op. cit.* p. 16.

16. Ainger tries to persuade himself that there was a tradition associating the Lollard, Oldcastle, with extreme fatness; but his editor, Beeching, is obliged to admit in a footnote that he is not aware of any references to this fatness before Shakespeare; *v.* Ainger, *op. cit.* pp. 126–30.

17. Cf. H. N. Hudson, *Shakespeare: his Life, Art and Characters* (ed. 1888), ii, p. 83: 'It must be no ordinary companionship that yields entertainment to such a spirit [as Prince Hal's] even in his loosest moments. Whatever

bad or questionable elements may mingle with his mirth, it must have some fresh and rich ingredients, some sparkling and generous flavour, to make him relish it. Anything like vulgar rowdyism cannot fail of disgusting him. His ears were never organised to that sort of music. Here then we have a sort of dramatic necessity for the character of Falstaff. To answer the purpose it was imperative that he should be just such a marvellous congregation of charms and vices as he is.' See also A. H. Tolman, *Falstaff and other Shakespearian Topics*, 1925, and W. W. Lawrence, *Shakespeare's Problem Comedies*, 1931, p. 64 (an interesting contrast between Hal and Falstaff, Bertram and Parolles).

18. *Poets and their Critics: Langland and Milton* (British Academy Warton Lecture), 1941, pp. 29–30.

19. *Oxford Lectures*, p. 256.   20. Pt. II, 4. 5. 131.

21. *V.* Pt. I, 2. 4. 107 (122): 'That damned brawn'; Pt. II, 1. 1. 19: 'Harry Monmouth's brawn'; 2. 2. 143 (159): 'Doth the old boar feed in the old frank? / At the old place, my lord, in Eastcheap'; and 2. 4. 224 (250): 'Thou whoreson little tidy Bartholomew boar-pig.'

22. Pt. I, 2. 2. 54 (59). This designation perhaps implies a claim to royal patronage on the proprietor's part, possibly connected with the quasi-historical incident known as the Hurling in Eastcheap, an affray which arose among their retinue while Hal's brothers, the princes John and Thomas, were taking supper at a tavern (unnamed) in Eastcheap, on St John's Eve, 1410, as is related by Stow (*v.* Kingsford, *op. cit.* p. xxxix).

23. *V.* 'East Cheap' in Sugden's *Topographical Dictionary to the Works of Shakespeare*.

24. *V.* note on *Piers Plowman*, Passus v, l. 313, ed. Skeat (Clarendon Press).

25. Pt. II, 2. 4. 11–12.   26. *Ibid.* 2. 1. 94 (102) ff.

27. Pt. I, 2. 4. 523–7 (584–90).   28. *Ibid.* 2. 4. 440 (497).

29. Pt. II, 2. 4. 59 (69).   30. Pt. I, 2. 4. 436 (494).

31. Pt. II, 2. 4. 59–61 (69–71).   32. Pt. I, 2. 2. 106 (115).

33. *Merry Wives of Windsor*, 3. 5. 103–12 (114–24).

34. Pt. I, 2. 4. 223 (252).   35. Pt. II, 1. 2. 155–61 (182–4).

36. *V. O.E.D.* 'gravy'.

37. *V.* p. 224, *Edinburgh University Journal*, Summer 1942 (art. on 'Shakespeare's Universe').

38. Pt. I, 1. 2. 131 (151); Pt. II, 2. 4. 211 (234).

39 Pt. I, 2. 4. 222, 252, 440 (251, 286, 498); *ibid.* 3. 3. 152, 155 (173, 176)

40. Pt. I, 3. 3. 176 (198).

41. Pt. I, 2. 4. 107 (122); Pt. II, 1. 1. 19.

42. Pt. II, 2. 2. 143 (169).   43. *Ibid.* 1. 2. 11–12 (13–14).

44. *Ibid.* 2. 4. 224–5 (250).   45. Pt. I, 2. 4. 441 (498).

46. Pt. II, 2. 2. 100 (110).

47. *V.* Sir E. K. Chambers, *Medieval Stage*, ch. XI, 'The Beginning of Winter'.

48. I owe this point to the late Lord Ernle: writing in *Shakespeare's England* (i, p. 356), he notes: 'To Shakespeare's mind the prodigious plenty of Martlemas suggested Falstaff in its proportions.'

49. *The Faerie Queene*, Bk. VII, canto vii, st. 40.

50. Pt. I, 5. 3. 57 (58).

51. George Meredith, *The Spirit of Shakespeare*.

52. *Characters of Shakespeare's Plays* (Hazlitt's *Works*, ed. A. R. Waller and A. Glover, 1902, i. 278).

53. Pt. I, 1. 2. 80–2, 90–6 (91–2, 102–10).

54. *Ibid.* 2. 4. 121–29 (137–47).   55. *V. supra*, p. 16 and ch. IV note 20.

56. *V.* p. xi of 1 *Henry IV*, ed. by G. L. Kittredge (Ginn & Co.). I fancy Hal is just a little tipsy at the beginning of Pt. I, 2. 4; but the point is, in general, sound enough, and the more striking that the chroniclers do not hide the fact that Prince Henry was given to sexual intemperance; *v.* Kingsford, *op. cit.* p. 17: 'he exercised meanelie the feates of Venus and of Mars, and other pastimes of youth, for so longe as the Kinge his father liued.'

57. Pt. I, 3. 3. 80–3 (90–3). 'The alternative title for the Prodigal Son was the "younger", as the alternative for the good brother was the "elder"' (Richmond Noble, *Shakespeare's Biblical Knowledge*, p. 277).

58. *The Merchant of Venice*, 2. 6. 14–19; cf. 3 *Henry VI*, 2. 1. 24: 'Trimmed like a younker, prancing to his love.'

59. Pt. I, 4. 2. 32–3 (37–9).

60. Cf. *As You Like It*, 3. 2. 271 (290): 'I answer you right painted cloth, from whence you have studied your questions.'

61. Pt. II, 2. 1. 143–7 (155–9).   62. *The Merry Wives*, 4. 5. 7.

III. THE BATTLE OF GAD'S HILL

1. *Lear*, 4. 1. 68. 'Lust-dieted' = with times and seasons regulated by his desires.

2. Cf. *Much Ado*, 2. 1. 126 (142), where Beatrice calls Benedick 'the prince's jester'.

3. John Bailey, *Shakespeare* ('English Heritage Series'), Longmans, 1929, p. 132.

4. Poins's age will, of course, be suggested by his make-up on the stage; one may best glean hints of Shakespeare's ideas about it from the scene which also tells us so much about his young master, i.e. 2 *Henry IV*, 2. 2.

5. *Twelfth Night*, 1. 5. 91 (103): 'There is no slander in an allowed fool, though he do nothing but rail.'

6. *V.* p. 124.

7. I.e. 2 *Henry IV*, 5. 1. 75 (85): 'I will devise matter enough out of this Shallow to keep Prince Harry in continual laughter the wearing out of six fashions', etc.

8. *V.* W. Creizenach, *The English Drama in the Age of Shakespeare*, Sidgwick & Jackson, 1916, pp. 273–5, and Granville-Barker on pp. 69–70, *A Companion to Shakespeare Studies*, 1934.

9. Cf. G. L. Kittredge, p. xi, Introd. to 1 *Henry IV* (Ginn & Co., 1940): 'This is, in effect, the author's explanation—a kind of chorus—and should be so understood. It is not the expression of the Prince's actual motive in upholding "the unyoked humour" of his riotous comrades. It amounts to a mere statement of fact made by Shakespeare himself: "When the Prince turns over a new leaf, he will be all the more admired for the contrast".' This well expresses the truth, though not, I think, quite the whole truth.

10. We are not actually told this until 1 *Henry IV*, 3. 2. 32–8. But the fact that even there the point is merely alluded to suggests that Shakespeare could assume the bulk of the audience to be familiar with it. Like the box on the ear given to the Lord Chief Justice, also treated allusively only, it was part of the legend, which everyone knew who knew anything at all about Prince Hal.

11. Bailey, *Shakespeare, op. cit.* p. 131.

12. Johnson's *Shakespeare*, iv, p. 123.   13. Charlton, *op. cit.* p. 169.

14. Sir Arthur Quiller-Couch, *op. cit.* p. 154.

15. Morgann, *op. cit.* pp. 4–5.   16. *Oxford Lectures*, p. 266.

17. Morgann, *op. cit.* p. 124; *Oxford Lectures*, p. 268 (footnote). Morgann attempts 'to account for and excuse' Falstaff's conduct on the absurd pretext that the sole testimony we have of the running and roaring is the word of the prejudiced Poins, that the Prince's comparison with the bull-calf two scenes later is merely a jesting exaggeration of Poins's statement, and that 'if he did roar for mercy, it must have been a very inarticulate sort of roaring, for there is not a single word set down

for Falstaff from which this roaring may be inferred'. Bradley faces the issue more squarely, as might be expected from so honest a critic, but with scarcely more courage. 'It is to be regretted', runs his footnote, 'that in carrying his guts away so nimbly he "roared for mercy"; for I fear we have no ground for rejecting Henry's statement to that effect, and I do not see my way to adopt the suggestion (I forget whose it is) that Falstaff spoke the truth when he swore that he knew Henry and Poins as well as he that made them.' The 'suggestion' he speaks of is, I think, H. N. Hudson's, *v. op. cit.* vol. ii, pp. 85–6.

18. Professor Kittredge (*op. cit.*) having made up his mind that 'Falstaff is not a coward in fact' gets rid of the roaring by declaring that Poins is here referring 'to the vociferous swaggering' as Falstaff attacks the travellers. Thus is a fine and independent judgement corrupted by romantic tradition. For nothing is more certain than that Poins's words at the end of 2. 2 and the Prince's about the bull-calf in 2. 4. 254 (287) refer to the same incident.

19. *Last Essays of Elia.*

20. Charlton, *op. cit.* p. 170; cf. Masefield, *Shakespeare*, p. 112.

21. Kittredge, *op. cit.* note on 2. 4. 77 (89): 'Away, you rogue!'

22. Pt. I, 2. 4. 10–14. 'Unlike the Prince, he is haughty to the drawers, who call him a proud Jack' (*Oxford Lectures*, p. 269).

23. Cf. Morgann, *op. cit.* p. 131: 'His entrance is delayed to stimulate our expectation.'

24. Pt. I, 1. 2. 178–82 (208–13).

25. Sir Thomas Palmer's lines prefixed to the folio ed. of Beaumont and Fletcher, 1647.

26. S. B. Hemingway, 1 *Henry IV* (A New Variorum Shakespeare), Lippincott, 1936, p. 144.

27. Kittredge's note is worth quotation here. Referring to Poins's weary 'Ay, ay, he said four', he writes:

'At about this point Falstaff (already suspicious) begins to feel pretty sure that the Prince has played him a trick. To test the matter, and to provide himself with a good answer if his suspicions come true, he raises the number of his alleged assailants with every breath. He does not expect Hal and Poins to believe him in these absurdities. Thus he is ready—when the Prince reveals the facts—to retort: "Why, I knew all that before!" with the implication: "and that's why I gave you such an absurd account of the whole affair. You might have guessed from my nonsensical story that I didn't expect you to believe me."'

Kittredge seems to treat the dialogue as if it occurred in a novel, and

I cannot see how this could all be made clear upon the stage. But we are agreed as to the point at which the lies become patently incredible.

28. I owe this point to Hemingway, *op. cit.* p. 145.

29. Cf. Hudson, *op. cit.* ii, p. 86. Hudson seems to have been the earliest critic to bring out the double purpose of Falstaff's lies. After quoting the passage about the knaves in Kendal green, he proceeds: 'These [lies], I take it, are studied self-exposures, to invite an attack. Else why should he thus affirm in the same breath the colour of the men's clothes and the darkness of the night? The whole thing is clearly a scheme to provoke his hearers to come down upon him, and then witch them with his facility and felicity in extricating himself. And so, when they pounce upon and seem to have him in their toils, he forthwith springs a diversion upon them.' If Hudson had meant by 'his hearers' the auditors in the theatre, not, as he does, the Prince and Poins, our views would be almost identical.

30. In suggesting this 'business' I follow an American stage-tradition, possibly derived from Samuel Phelps, *v.* Brander Matthews, *Shakesperian Stage Traditions*, p. 11 (cited by Hemingway).

31. *Life of Johnson*, ed. Birkbeck Hill, iii. 69.

32. *V. supra*, p. 40.

33. Cf. *Oxford Lectures*, p. 267: 'When the Sheriff came to the inn to arrest him for an offence whose penalty was death, Falstaff, who was hidden behind the arras, did not stand there quaking for fear, he immediately fell asleep and snored.'

34. In Pt. II, 2. 4. 320 (352) the Prince charges Falstaff with defaming Mistress Tearsheet out of 'pure fear and entire cowardice'. But it is, I think, clear that here Sir John's evasion, in so far as it is not intended as a mere display of dexterity, is due rather to policy than to physical fear.

IV. THE PRINCE GROWS UP

1. Pt. II, 4. 4. 118–20.   2. Pt. I, 3. 2. 156.
3. *Ibid.* 3. 2. 32–5.
4. Peter Alexander, *Shakespeare's Life and Art*, 1938, p. 120.
5. Pt. II, 2. 2.   6. *Oxford Lectures*, p. 258.
7. Such anticipation follows, it should be noted, the time-honoured practice of the old religious plays; cf. the comic scene of *The Second Shepherd's Play*, in which the shepherds present their gifts to Mak's wife and the supposed child, which immediately precedes that in which offerings are made to the Holy Child.   8. Pt. I, 5. 1. 94.

9. Pt. I, 4. 1. 94–110.   10. *Ibid.* 5. 2. 53 ff.

11. See the article by H. Hartman, *Pub. Mod. Lang. Assoc.* 1931.

12. Pt. I, 5. 4. 96 ff.

13. H. N. Hudson, as usual, is the only critic to see the facts; cf. *infra*, ch. v, 32 note.   14. Pt. I, 3. 2. 139.

15. *Ibid.* 4. 1. 10.   16. *Ibid.* 1. 3. 201 ff.

17. *Henry V*, 4. 3. 28–9.   18. *Ibid.* ll. 57–62.

19. What I have written in the preceding paragraphs may be compared with the following passage from H. N. Hudson, *op. cit.* vol. ii, p. 123:

'No sooner had Prince Henry slain the valiant Percy than he fell at once to doing him the offices of pious and tender reverence; and the rather, forasmuch as no human eye witnessed the act. He knew that the killing of Hotspur would be enough of itself to wipe out all his shames, and "restore him unto the good thoughts of the world again"; nevertheless he cheerfully resigned the credit of the deed to Falstaff. He knew that such a surreptitious honour would help his old companion in the way wherein he was most capable and needy of help; while, for himself, he could forego the fame of it in the secret pledge it gave him of other and greater achievements: the inward conscience thereof sufficed him; and the sense of having done a generous thing was dearer to him than the beguiling sensation of "riding in triumph on men's tongues". This noble superiority to the breath of present applause is what most clearly evinces the solidity and inwardness of his virtue.

'Yet in one of his kingliest moments he tells us, "If it be a sin to covet honour, I am the most offending soul alive." But honour is with him in the highest sense a social conscience, and the rightful basis of self-respect: he deems it a good chiefly as it makes a man clean and strong within, and not as it dwells in the fickle breath of others. As for that conventional figment which small souls make so much ado about, he cares little for it, as knowing that it is often got without merit, and lost without deserving. Thus the honour he covets is really to deserve the good thoughts of men: the inward sense of such desert is enough: if what is fairly his due in that kind be withheld by them, the loss is theirs, not his.'

I was the more struck by these views that, before coming upon them, I had arrived at the closely similar ones, set forth above. Hudson is, I think, the only critic in the nineteenth century to do full justice to the character of Prince Hal; Dowden's appreciation, which is far slighter, being evidently indebted to him.

20. My evidence is *The Famous Victories of Henry the Fifth*, a much debased version, as I believe, of the two old plays that lie behind the three Shakespearian plays, *Henry IV* (I and II) and *Henry V*. In this we have no scene in which the Lord Chief Justice gets his ears boxed, but a comic rehearsal or reproduction of such a scene by two clowns, which suggests that it formed part of the original drama.

21. Pt. II, 2. 2. 54–8 (60–4).   22. *Ibid.* 2. 2. 170–3 (192–6).
23. *Ibid.* 4. 4. 30–5.   24. *Ibid.* 4. 4. 56–66.
25. *Ibid.* 4. 5. 22–3.   26. *Ibid.* 4. 5. 167–9.
27. *Ibid.* 4. 5. 43–7.   28. *Ibid.* 4. 5. 102–3.
29. *Ibid.* 4. 5. 120–38.

V. FALSTAFF HIGH ON FORTUNE'S WHEEL

1. Cf. *supra*, p. 2, and Stoll, *Shakespeare Studies*, p. 428: 'To this type [the braggart captain] Falstaff unquestionably belongs.' The *Trans. of the Royal Soc. of Literature*, vol. xix, contains an interesting and useful survey of 'The Soldier in English Drama' by Dr F. S. Boas, who, I am glad to note, writes: 'Sir John is far too complex and dazzling a creation to be ranked with the braggart soldier type' (p. 132).

2. This is one of Maurice Morgann's flashes of genius (*v.* p. 100). Cf. also his p. 134: 'His braggadocioes...are braggadocioes *after the fact*. In other cases we see the Coward of the Play bluster and boast for a time, talk of distant wars and private duels...till at length, on the proof of some present and apparent fact he is brought to open and *lasting* shame.... But in the instance before us every thing is reversed: The Play opens with the *Fact*.... This Fact is preceded by no bluster or pretence whatever; the lies and braggadocioes follow,' etc.

3. Pt. I, 3. 3. 185 (209) ff.
4. *Winter's Tale*, 4. 4. 668 (687).   5. Pt. II, 3. 2. 289 (312).
6. *V. The Army* by J. W. Fortescue in *Shakespeare's England*, i, pp. 112–13, 122–5.
7. *V.* Arden ed. of 1 *Henry IV*, note on 5. 3. 36, which quotes Sir John Smythe, *Certain Discourses Militarie*, 1590, and *v.* also Hemingway, *op. cit.* p. 313.   8. *Oxford Lectures*, p. 267.
9. Arden ed. *op. cit.*, which also quotes T. Powell, *Tom of all Trades*, 1631 (ed. Furnivall, pp. 169–70), etc.

10. Pt. II, 2. 1. 188 (199).   11. Pt. I, 4. 2. 78–9 (85–6).
12. Pt. II, 4. 3. 26–9 (29–32).   13. Pt. I, 5. 4. 120.
14. *Ibid.* 5. 3. 57–60.   15. *Oxford Lectures*, p. 267.

16. Pt. I, 2. 4. 357–63 (402–7).   17. *V. supra*, pp. 70–1.

18. Cf. Stoll, *op. cit.* p. 432: 'Falstaff goes to war to furnish matter for comedy, the Prince gives him a charge to get him to the war, and the dozen captains come sweating to fetch the luxurious laggard to his charge.'

19. *Oxford Lectures*, p. 267, and cf. note 14.

20. *V.* Pt. I, 3. 3. 185 (208). Falstaff underlines the bare adequacy of this charge by complaining that he has not been given a charge of horse.

21. *V. supra*, p. 4.   22. *V. supra*, p. 68.

23. Pt. II, 1. 2. 147 (167).   24. *Ibid.* 1. 1. 19.

25. Morgann, *op. cit.* p. 42.   26. Pt. II, 1. 1. 19–20.

27. *Ibid.* 2. 4. 352–4 (387–9).

28. *Ibid.* 2. 4. 366 (401). Cf. ll. 369–71 (405–7). The summons, as Stoll suggests (*v.* note 18), is really to answer for neglect of duty, but Falstaff had been entrusted with some special charge (Pt. II, 1. 2. 63 (72)), and the whereabouts of a mere captain could not be supposed to have occasioned all this fuss at headquarters.

29. Pt. II, 3. 2. 55 (61) ff.   30. *Ibid.* 4. 3. 16 (18) ff.

31. Morgann, *op. cit.* p. 104.

32. H. N. Hudson (*op. cit.* vol. i, pp. 305–6) alone seems to have noted a connection between Falstaff's claims at Shrewsbury and the development of his character in Part II. His observations have been generally overlooked, and are not even quoted in the American Variorum, because, I think, in his usual unsystematic way, he prints them, not under *Henry IV*, but as a digression to his treatment of *The Merry Wives*, which belongs to another volume. It was, indeed, by the merest chance that I happened upon them, at a late stage of this enquiry. I quote the relevant passage which, though a little heavy-handed on the moral side, after the nineteenth-century fashion, brings out the dramatic facts well enough.

'At the close of the First Part of the History, the Prince freely yields up to him the honour of Hotspur's fall; thus carrying home to him such an example of self-renouncing generosity as it would seem impossible for the most hardened sinner to resist. And the Prince appears to have done this partly in the hope that it might prove a seed of truth and grace in Falstaff, and start him in a better course of life. [This seems to be a mis-interpretation of Hal's words "if a lie may *do thee grace*" (Pt. I, 5. 4. 156 (161)); whereas "do thee grace" actually means "win thee favour". J. D. W.] But the effect upon him is quite the reverse. Honour is nothing to him but as it may help him in the matter of sensual and heart-steeling self-indulgence. And the surreptitious fame thus acquired, instead of working in him for good, merely serves to procure him larger means and larger license for pampering his gross animal selfishness. His thoughts dwell not at all on the Prince's act of magnanimity, which would shame his egotism and soften his heart, but only on his own ingenuity and success in the stratagem that led to that act. So that the effect is just to puff him up more than ever with vanity and conceit of wit, and thus to give a looser rein and a sharper stimulus to his greed and lust; for there is probably nothing that will send a man faster to the Devil than that sort of conceit. The result is, that Falstaff soon proceeds to throw off whatever of restraint may have hitherto held his vices in check, and to wanton in the arrogance of utter impunity. As he then unscrupulously appropriated the credit of another's heroism, so he now makes no scruple of sacrificing the virtue, the honour, the happiness of others to his own mean and selfish pleasure.'

In the latter part of this Hudson writes with *The Merry Wives* rather than 2 *Henry IV* in mind.

33. Pt. I, 5. 4. 139–40 (143–7).

34. *Ibid.* 5. 4. 161–4 (166–9). 'Follow for reward' is a hunting-cry to the hounds at the end of the chase, the 'reward' being the portions assigned to them at the 'breaking-up of the deer' (*v.* Turbervile, *Booke of Hunting*, 1576, pp. 132–5). Falstaff is the hound that has brought down the great quarry.

35. Pt. II, 1. 2. 1–5, 115–16 (133).

36. Pt. I, 1. 3. 30 ff. The popinjay's pouncet-box was used for purposes of disinfection; he was also well seen in remedies 'for an inward bruise'.

37. *Book of Homage to Shakespeare*, p. 150.

38. *Oxford Lectures*, pp. 261–2.

39. Pt. II, 1. 2. 6 ff.

40. *Ibid.* 1. 2. 210 (238) ff.

41. *Oxford Lectures*, p. 271.

42. *Ibid.* p. 273.

43. *Ibid.* pp. 272–3.

44. *V.* note 32 above.

45. There are hints of them, however, in Charlton's fine study of the fat knight's character.

46. Cf. Pt. II, 1. 2. 201–4 (227–30):

L. C. Justice. Well, the king hath severed you: I hear you are going with Lord John of Lancaster against the Archbishop and the Earl of Northumberland.

Falstaff. Yea, I thank your pretty sweet wit for it.

47. *V. Review of English Studies*, xvii, pp. 389–90:

'In *Henry IV, Pt. II* the Lord Chief Justice stands as an embodiment of everything that's excellent, and clearly represents civil law. He is the real antagonist of Falstaff, and it is he whom King Henry V admits as "a father to my youth" (5. 2. 118) after the judge has made his noble defence of his own act in committing to prison "the immediate heir of England" (5. 2. 73 ff.). This adoption seals the doom of Falstaff, the grey-haired iniquity, who was even then saying "the laws of England are at my commandment. Blessed are they that have been my friends, and woe to my lord chief justice".'

48. *Oxford Lectures*, pp. 270–1.

49. Hudson, *op. cit.* ii. p. 91. Hudson, like the rest, misses the function of the Lord Chief Justice.

50. Pt. II, 2. 1. 114 (126) ff.

51. Johnson's *Shakespeare*, iv, p. 356.

52. Pt. I, 2. 4. 394–7 (445–9).

53. *Ibid.* 3. 3. 136 (155).

54. *Oxford Lectures*, pp. 251–2.

55. Pt. II, 2. 2. 107–32 (129–46).

56. Herford and Simpson, *Ben Jonson*, vol. i, p. 194.

57. *Oxford Lectures*, p. 264.

58. Pt. II, 2. 4. 91–4 (105–9).

59. I depart here from the traditional interpretation which, following a stage-direction of Rowe's, makes Falstaff drive Pistol from the room. It seems to me clear from the dialogue that while Falstaff puts up a brave show, accompanied apparently by shouts (as at Gad's Hill) even after Pistol has been disposed of (cf. Doll's 'I prithee, Jack, be quiet, the rascal is gone'), the real business of expulsion is done by Bardolph.

60. *Ibid.* 5. 4. 5: 'She shall have whipping-cheer enough, I warrant her. There hath been a man or two lately killed about her', and ll. 18–19: 'The man is dead that you and Pistol beat amongst you.'

61. Morgann, *op. cit.* pp. 178–82. Cf. Hudson, *op. cit.* ii, pp. 98–9: 'His abuse of Shallow's hospitality is exceedingly detestable, and argues that hardening of all within which tells far more against a man than almost any amount of mere sensuality....The bad usage which Falstaff puts upon Shallow has the effect of justifying to us the usage which he at last receives from the Prince.'

62. Pt. II, 5. 1. 43–7 (51–5).

63. *V.* Cheyney, *History of England*, ii, ch. XXXVII.

64. *Henry IV, Pt. II*, ed. by C. H. Herford, 1928 ('Warwick Shakespeare'), p. 121.

65. Pt. II, 5. 3. 39–42.

VI. THE CHOICE AND THE BALANCE

1. Pt. II, 5. 1. 75–83 (85–94).
2. Cf. *What happens in 'Hamlet'*, pp. 264–5.
3. Pt. II, 5. 3. 133–41 (135–45).   4. *Oxford Lectures*, pp. 258–9.
5. *V.* Cheyney, *History of England*, ii, pp. 75, 77.
6. *Henry IV, Pt. II*, ed. by R. P. Cowl (1923), Introd. pp. xxix–xxx.
7. *Oxford Lectures*, p. 253.   8. *Ibid.* p. 253.
9. *V. supra*, p. 77.   10. *Oxford Lectures*, p. 253.
11. *Ibid.* p. 254.
12. *V.* Johnson's *Shakespeare*, iv, pp. 352–3.
13. *Oxford Lectures*, p. 254.   14. Pt. II, 5. 2. 78.
15. Ed. 1709, p. xviii.
16. Johnson, *op. cit.* iv, p. 353.
17. *Henry V*, 2. 1. 117; 2. 3. 9–25.
18. Swinburne, *A Study of Shakespeare*, pp. 106–7.
19. *Oxford Lectures*, pp. 252–3.

20. *V.* pp. 265–7 of his article in *The Mod. Lang. Review*, vol. xxv. But for Malone I think historians of the stage might long since have assumed that Kempe was probably cast for Falstaff. Malone makes two statements on the matter, both of doubtful relevancy. He first suggests that Kempe played Shallow in 2 *Henry IV*, his reason being that the character called 'Kempe' in 2 *Return from Parnassus*, a student-play acted at St John's, Cambridge, about Christmas, 1601–2, after declaring to another character, Philomusus, that he would make an apt pupil to himself, remarks 'and your face me thinkes would be good for a foolish mayre or a foolish justice of peace' (*v.* Boswell's ed. of *Malone's Shakespeare*, 1821, 2 *Henry IV*, 3. 3 note, and Macray, *Parnassus Plays*, p. 100). This seems a flimsy basis for supposing that Kempe played Shallow. And Malone's other statement, that Heminge 'is said to have been the original performer of Falstaff' is scarcely more satisfactory, since (i) the only authority he cites is 'some tract of which I forgot to preserve the title', and (ii) the lost reference, if otherwise satisfactory, may have referred to the Falstaff of *The Merry Wives*, which was first played about 1600 or 1601, after Kempe had left the company.

21. *V.* notes on 2. 4 of 2 *Henry IV* in the forthcoming edition of 'The New Shakespeare'.

22. *V.* J. Q. Adams, *Shakespearean Playhouses*, p. 240.

23. Unhappily as a resident in Scotland I found myself debarred from witnessing Mr Robert Atkins's recent production of 2 *Henry IV* at the

Westminster Theatre. I gather, however, from a notice by Mr Desmond MacCarthy (*New Statesman*, 5 December 1942) that Mr Atkins made his final exit with 'a bowed head and a quick heavy stride'. How this was reconciled with Shakespeare's text, in which Falstaff's last utterance is the interrupted protest, 'My lord, my lord—', as the officers hurry him from the stage, I cannot say. But it looks as if Mr Atkins had Bradley's article and the death-bed scene in view. Certainly, Mr MacCarthy had; for he complains that Mr Atkins 'failed to make the utmost of Falstaff's crushing discomfiture'.

24. Cf. H. T. Rötscher, *Shakespeare in seinen höchsten Charaktergebilden enthüllt und entwickelt*, Dresden, 1864. I have been unable to see Rötscher in the original, but there is a paraphrase in A. Ralli's *Shakespearian Criticism*, i. 440.

25. The actual sum was 300 marks or £200 (*v.* 2. 1. 54; 2. 4. 508), but it assumes the epical proportion of £1000 in Falstaff's mind immediately after he loses it (*v.* 2. 4. 156).

26. Cf. Charlton, *op. cit.* pp. 188–207. I must confess that, while admiring the many happy touches in its general drift, I find this argument difficult to follow.

27. *Oxford Lectures*, p. 252. This is the feeling Bradley admits we might have had but for the imprisonment at the Fleet and the death in *Henry V*.

28. *The Essential Shakespeare*, pp. 88–9; cf. the remarks of John Bailey, cited above, pp. 9–10.

29. *V. Aspects of Shakespeare* (British Academy), 1933, pp. 227 ff. For Abercrombie's 'free' interpretation of *Henry IV*, *v.* p. 246.